Police Ethics:
A Matter of Character

Douglas W. Perez
Plattsburgh State University, New York

J. Alan Moore
Champlain College of Vermont

THOMSON

WADSWORTH

Dedication

For Our Children

The Perezs: Annie and Elizabeth

and

The Moores: Dylan, Maria, and Michaéla

ISBN 13: 978-1-928-91622-2
ISBN: 1-928916-22-8
Library of Congress Catalog Number: 2002102064

Thomson Higher Education
10 Davis Drive
Belmont, CA 94002-3098
USA

For information about our products, contact us:
Thomson Learning Academic Resource Center
1-800-423-0563
http://www.wadsworth.com

For permission to use material from this text or product, submit a request online at http://www.thomsonrights.com

Any additional questions about permissions can be submitted by email to thomsonrights@thomson.com

Printed in the United States of America
10 9 8 7 6 5 4

Contents

Part 1

The Setting   15

Chapter 1

The New Police Professionalism   17

Chapter 2

Why Be Ethical?   31

Part 2

Ethical Frameworks   43

Chapter 3

Chapter 4

Chapter 5

Chapter 6

Chapter 7

Chapter 8

Judgment Calls   113

Part 3

Applications   125

Chapter 9

Types of Police Misconduct   127

Chapter 10

Corruption of Authority and Police Crime   141

Chapter 11

Chapter 12

Part 4

Implications   181

Chapter 13

Chapter 14

Acknowledgments

First, we would like to thank the director of the Institute for Ethics in Public Life, Tom Moran, and the fellows at the institute. The concepts included in this work have been polished and enhanced by the ideas and reflections of everyone there. The appointment to the institute allowed us a freedom to read, reflect, and write on these subjects that would not otherwise have been possible.

Second, we wish to acknowledge the many hours of editing and discussion that were contributed by our group of loyal reviewers. Tom Moran took time off from his busy schedule running the institute to review preliminary drafts. Jim Godfrey, full-time police officer and coach, took many hours out of his days and nights to do the same. Jeanne Zimmerman's insight and careful eye for editing were immensely helpful. And Betsy Zumwalt Perez, though a dilettante in our field, took time to edit numerous drafts and to give us an "outsider's" perspective.

Rita Latour, the departmental secretary for Sociology and Criminal Justice, was our savior on many occasions. Her typing skills and dedication to helping the project reach fruition hastened the completion of the work by several months at least.

This book has been put together after several decades of working with police officers. Through their examples, many officers and police leaders have contributed to the work, albeit indirectly. That is, by being modern professionals, by exhibiting their competence and insight, and by courageously embracing the challenges of police work in an ethical way, they have influenced the work's substance profoundly. John Gackowski, Skip Stevens, and Dick Rainey of the Contra Costa County (California) Sheriff's Department come to mind. Jim Simonson and Nolan Darnell of the Oakland (California) Police Department and Al Salerno of the Berkeley (California) Police Department equally have made pronounced contributions to our understanding of ethical policing.

Finally, there are the police leaders it has been our privilege to know and to work with who have also driven this work by their examples. Chief George Hart of Oakland P.D., Chief Dashel Butler of Berkeley P.D., Chief Kevin Scully of Burlington (Vermont) P.D., and Chief John Terry of Essex Junction (Vermont) P.D. have been sources of inspiration and, at times, lights in the dark forest.

To all these people, we owe our thanks. If this work is effective in accomplishing its appointed task, in making a difference on the streets of America, it will be a testimony to all of them.

Please note: we don't want you getting lost as you move between the Web and print formats, so we numbered the primary heads and subheads in each chapter the same. For example, the first primary head in Chapter 1 is labeled 1-1, the second primary head in this chapter is labeled 1-2, and so on. The subheads build from the designation of their corresponding primary head: 1-1a, 1-1b, etc.

The numbering system is designed to make moving between the online and print versions as seamless as possible. So if your instructor tells you to read the material in 2-3 and 2-4 for tomorrow's assignment, you'll know that the information appears in Chapter 2 of both the Web and print versions of the text, and you can then choose the best way for you to complete the assignment.

Introduction

"You treat everyone the same, kid. You're civil to everyone and cordial to no one ... everyone deserves some amount of respect, but no one deserves courtesy ... That's 'Kilvinsky's Law.'"

— Veteran Officer Kilvinsky
(Speaking to a rookie in the movie *The New Centurions*)

Outline

Our title may suggest an open invitation to police officers to be egocentric, to do whatever they feel is appropriate on duty, and to avoid taking the rule of law seriously. We appear to be saying that the rule of cop is what's important because, on the street, what police officers say goes. We seem, in other words, to be confirming a police locker room idea that we (the police) are the law and that to operate on this basis is at once realistic and morally defensible.

Is that what we mean by our title? Because they make thousands of important, life-changing decisions every day, often alone and unsupervised, is it true that the police are the law?

I-1 Street Justice

The answer is both yes and no. On the one hand, the police must apply the law fairly, evenhandedly, and with a view to promote justice. Laws are created by legislatures that pass them in the name, and presumably in the best interests, of all of the people. The police cannot think or act as if they are completely free, by themselves, to define legal and illegal, to decide who are inherently good people and who are inherently bad people, or to rule the streets as an occupying army. This is exactly what the police do in police states against which America has fought a number of wars. In such countries, the police have so much power that the law, as written, is largely irrelevant to the lives of millions of people. Citizens in these countries are subject to the whims of absolute police power and, in a sense, are victimized by the "law."

Ours is a country of laws and of constitutional principles, the sole purpose of which is to create a society where everybody is free to pursue what he or she, individually, believes is the good in life. This ideal of our system rests on the understanding that there is no such thing as a single good or best way to live for all people. The definition of what counts as "good" is highly divisive and highly individualized.

The idea of a "good life," a life that is personally satisfying and meaningful, is the dominant motivation in the life of most any person. The pursuit of the things that make life good, or better, makes up a person's life story. This pursuit is the organizing principle of a person's "story line." It is what makes a person's behavior understandable. In other words, what counts as good for a person (having a family, getting an education, making a lot of money, etc.), and the way one pursues that good (being loyal, going to college, getting a good job, etc.), form the basis that defines his or her individuality.

Justice provides the environment within which the pursuit of the good is possible. We will talk more about justice later (in chapter 3), but for now we will suggest two concepts to consider. First, let us consider justice to be "fairness" in the general sense of the term. When justice is successful, people are treated fairly relative to each other. Second, let us also consider justice to be the Greek notion that it is the kind of balance that prevails in life when "each is given his or her due." That is, justice involves allocating resources and rights in a way that allows individuals to obtain what it is that they are due, what they deserve, in a moral sense.

When the police act, they must understand this underlying concept, and they must behave in a way that does honor to it. Thus, the streets of America must be ruled by laws that are applied fairly. While the law treats people differently because of their behavior (sanctioning them when they perpetrate crimes), it cannot (in an ethically or legally defensible way) treat people in different ways because of their personal characteristics (such as race, religion, manner of dress, political views, etc.). Thus, from this perspective, the law is absolute.

On the other hand, to a great extent, the actions of the police do, in fact, determine what the law really means. The police put practical application into the American legal system. If the laws the police uphold are the skeleton, then the on-the-street discretionary decisions of the police put flesh and blood on that skeleton. The police make the written laws of the penal code come to life for the public. See box I-1.

We intend to confirm what a number of analysts and well-informed, intuitive police officers have pointed out for a very long time—that no matter what the law states, no matter how penal code sections read, no matter what training teaches, and no matter what police leadership may want to tell us, the true meaning of the law on the streets is determined by police officers.

When officers decide on a day-to-day basis where to focus their attention, whom to arrest, and when to use force, they determine the effects the legal system will have on the lives of individual citizens. This means police officers bear a tremendous and unique responsibility. If they either overlook or overemphasize certain types of crimes, they can (effectively) change the criminal law. If, for example, in a college town the police look the other way when college kids are involved in underage drinking, then underage drinking has, in effect, been decriminalized in that town. If the police in one jurisdiction decide not to worry too much about local gambling rooms, then gambling has been (again, effectively) decriminalized there.

Box I-1

Curbside Justice—The Exercise of Absolute Police Power

In 1966 in Spain, dictator Generalisimo Francisco Franco was in power. The police, specifically the national police (the *Guardia Civil*), exercised absolute power over individual citizens. One day that summer, at a bullfight in Madrid, a young, starving, peasant boy was detained for trying to steal the purse of an American tourist. Instead of taking the boy out of the arena and to jail, two officers—each weighing in excess of two hundred pounds—marched the boy (who weighed under one hundred pounds) around the arena, beating him with their nightsticks. The beating continued for about five minutes until the boy was covered in blood and unconscious. He was then dragged from the arena.

The American woman/victim, who first called for the police, was in tears by the time the altercation was over. She felt that she had caused this small, poor boy to be killed. Being an American, she felt ashamed of herself for not understanding what the consequences would be of reporting such a petty theft to the police in totalitarian Spain. She later said that she would have given the boy her purse if she had known what was going to happen to him. The woman left Spain vowing never to return to "such a country."

While the Spanish police were not technically within their rights to exact such an on-the-street punishment for a minor offense, it was clear that they knew they would never be questioned and never be sanctioned for this conduct. Indeed, the crowd at the bullring remained completely silent through-out the entire incident. Knowing the absolute power of the police, these Spaniards feared that other members of the *Guardia Civil* (clearly evident throughout the arena) would treat them to a dose of such curbside justice if they protested.

When the police make such decisions in response to local pressures (to "leave the college kids alone, they pay the bills in this town"), they might be making perfectly rational public policy decisions. But by avoiding the dictates of the law in this and a thousand other ways, the police can create the impression that police practices are arbitrary, preferential, or biased. Such impressions promote cynicism among citizens and thereby alienate citizens from the criminal justice system.

These two examples—ignoring underage drinking and gambling—involve the police deciding not to invoke the law. But the police can, equally, appear to be guilty of unfairness and arbitrariness by applying the law rigorously. If, for example, the police decide that, in an effort to thwart the growth of local gangs, they will stop every teenage driver to make records and warrants checks, ask for information, and generally make things uncomfortable for gang members—then the police have effectively created a new, separate set of unique laws that apply to one segment of the population.

In these ways, the discretionary decisions of the police, to arrest or not to arrest, to use force or not to use force, to treat details as criminal matters or as service calls, all determine the real impact of the law. Thus, in a practical sense, it often matters little what is written on paper and stored on a shelf in a law library under "State Penal Code." When the police use their discretionary decision-making powers to emphasize or de-emphasize one type of criminal behavior or another, they control what the real law is on the street. In a truer sense, then, the impact of the entire criminal justice system is determined by street justice.

It is imperative that police officers understand they possess this power and, in order to use it wisely, understand how critical it is that they possess a personal ethic that is morally and legally defensible. It is around this principal theme that we have built this book.

Individual police officers often have to make most of their decisions without supervision and with no direction to follow other than what is in their own minds and in their own hearts. For all practical purposes, no one is there to hold them accountable when they decide whether or not to stop a vehicle. No one can effectively monitor in real-time how respectful, civil, and decent the individual officer is when dealing with citizens or—and this is especially important—how often the officer decides not to take action. These are some of the unavoidable realities of police work.

The idea behind this book is to emphasize the full importance of police ethics. If an officer is corrupt, unfair, prejudiced, and/or driven by personal vendettas, then so is that officer's "law." If officers are honest, sufficiently educated, and controlled by a desire to apply the law in a fair way to all people, then the law will be a tool for the maintenance of justice. There is no way around this reality. How officers use discretion is of absolute importance to their communities, to the criminal justice system, and to America itself. Put bluntly, the decisions of the police define justice, in both of the senses that we discussed above—justice as fairness (equal treatment) and justice in terms of the distribution of what people deserve. See box I-2.

We are going to discuss the idea that a critical factor in police competence is ethical judgement. Furthermore, officer discretion is driven by the character of individual officers. To be a competent, professional police officer involves making wise judgements about people, situations, and the applicability of the law. Because police fix the limits of the law on the

Box I-2

Two Definitions of "Justice"

1. Justice as Process: Justice prevails when people under similar circumstances are treated in an equal and fair manner before the law.

2. Justice as Substance: Justice prevails when people receive from the law what they deserve to receive.

street, their ethical judgement, and thus their competence, is crucial to determining whether or not the legal system dispenses justice. Police ethics are not and cannot be considered something separate from police competence.

We will consider several classical theories of ethics and develop our own character-based ethic for police officers, "an ethic to live by," by combining the strengths of these theories. We will spend some time applying this ethic to the challenges and issues police officers face every day. Our intent is to bring to the reader an appreciation for the centrality of ethics in everyday police work. This will help not only to create an attitude about professionalism among police officers but will also help to generate a respect for law and for the police among citizens. Nothing could be more important for us all in contemporary American society.

One final note is important, and it sets up a number of frustrating realities for the police and for anyone who is concerned about police accountability. The duties that police are supposed to accomplish and the roles that they are supposed to play are multiple, conflicting, and vague (see box I-3). There is no one, single thing the police are supposed to do and no one, single role they are supposed to play. On the street, there is a constant struggle to get multiple jobs done using many varied tools while at the same time playing numerous roles.

Analysts agree that the police have three basic sets of functions and roles, those of law enforcement, order maintenance, and service. An ongoing reality of police work, and a frustrating one at that, is that these functions/roles are rather vague. For example, what do we mean by "maintaining order"? Doesn't making arrests (law enforcement) contribute to order maintenance? Doesn't finding a lost child (service) help to maintain the social order? This vagueness in definition creates confusion about what the police are supposed to do and about how to prioritize any analysis of what they are really doing.

Box I-3

Multiple, Conflicting, and Vague Functions

The three major functions of the police, which are admittedly vague and often in conflict with each other, are to:

- Enforce the Law
- Maintain Order
- Provide Community Services

When should the police focus on maintaining order, when should they be service oriented, and when should they be enforcing the law? It is clear that a homicide requires law enforcement, unruly crowds require order maintenance, and a traffic accident requires a service orientation. But, in fact, these three functions/roles can conflict with each other. When they do (and they often do), the police are left to make up their own rules using their discretionary decision-making powers.

The classic conflict between these functions/roles involves decisions about what the police should do when confronted with lawlessness that, if dealt with as a legal issue, could turn into large-scale disorder. For example, the police will sometimes observe drug use at a huge, orderly rock concert, or they will deal with a large group of underage drinkers at an otherwise calm and controlled fraternity party. To enforce the letter of the law on such occasions might very well involve creating major crowd control problems—problems for the police that could easily be avoided by ignoring the absolute dictates of the law. Enforcing the law (making or attempting to make arrests) under such circumstances is in direct conflict with order maintenance.

Such details are not unusual in police work. Thus, the multiple, conflicting, and vague nature of what the police do and what they are supposed to do colors every day on the street in a profound way. It sometimes creates confusion for the police, distrust of the police, and difficulties that directly impact our discussion of what ethical conduct is and how the police can be held to answer for their conduct. We will revisit this "multiple, conflicting, and vague" notion a number of times throughout this book.

I-2 The Need for Ethics Study by the Police

When people think about the study of ethics, they often think about the ancient Greeks and discussions about philosophy. Historically, police officers have been particularly prone to think that philosophy has nothing to do with real life on the street. The authors believe this is not only wrong, but that this impression severely limits the development of police competence and character. Why is it so important for the police officer today to become involved in discussions about morality that are more than two thousand years old? The answer comes in several parts.

I-2a Limited Police Academy Training in Ethics

First, police academies, even with today's sophisticated and broadly based curriculum, include very little in the way of the study of ethics. A nationwide survey found that state regulations require an average of only three and one-half hours of ethics training in an entire police academy experience. Thus, the amount of time spent debating, analyzing, and studying the sort of ethical dilemmas that are regularly encountered by police officers is very small. Given the gravity of the problem of police misconduct and the opportunities and enticements to misbehave faced by every officer on the street, this amount of discussion is woefully inadequate.

But there is more to this problem. In addition to insufficient time, the type of discussion police cadets in academies experience with regard to ethics is also inadequate. In most places, police academy ethics discussions involve nothing more than lectures given by someone from internal affairs (IA) about what police officers should not do when they hit the street. These "lists of do's and don'ts" are often disregarded by cadets who already possess some police subcultural cynicism about IA. Discussions about how a cop can get into trouble tend to fall on deaf ears.

What is missing is an approach to the subject from the ground up. It is obviously worthwhile to teach recruits how to avoid getting into trouble. But such a negative approach cannot be taken alone. To focus exclusively on how to avoid getting into trouble implies that to be a good, competent police officer merely involves not making mistakes. This idea is problematic because it distorts what is meant by police competence and the positive duties involved in being a professional officer—a person who possesses and exhibits good character.

Discussing examples of what police officers should not do ought to be engaged as an aspect of the larger issue of what competent, professional police officers should be. A systematic treatment of ethics, even if it is abbreviated, is necessary to make the connection between a police officer's duty and the common good of the community.

I-2b Limited Academic Training in Ethics

There is another reason to emphasize the study of ethics in the world of policing. An increasing number of police recruits have college experience behind them, and many major in criminal justice. Existing criminal justice ethics classes tend to discuss ethics from the positive perspective that we are suggesting. They start with philosophical considerations of ethics in general and move through analyses of what it means to be a professional police officer. As opposed to the treatment accorded ethics in police academies, this is a much more appropriate way to deal with such a complex subject.

The problem is that many colleges don't offer criminal justice ethics classes at all. At lower-division community colleges in particular, such classes are either missing or are seldom taught. Also, most college programs don't require students who are pre-law enforcement to take a course in ethics. Thus, even though such programs offer good classes on the subject, most officers today are never engaged in the type of thoughtful analysis of personal character and police ethics that is necessary to be an officer in the twenty-first century.

I-2c The Intellectual Capabilities of Today's Officer

A third reason for studying ethics in this manner is because today's modern police officer is equipped with the intelligence and education to engage in such discussions.

This is not to say that the police officers of the past were not honest, hard working, committed people. But it does mean that today we no longer presume police officers cannot understand discussions about the principles of philosophy, of good character, or of ethical conduct. Today's officers can approach ethics from an informed perspective, and it is critical they do so. In a time when community-based policing (CBP) is expanding the power possessed by individual officers on the street, police officers' personal ethical frames of reference are more and more important (this will be discussed more completely in chapter 1).

So, there is no doubt that today's officers can engage in analytical discussions about police ethics. The question is, do they want to? Why, for example, should police officers want to debate the principles of being a good person that were outlined by Aristotle more than two thousand years ago? The answer is: these principles are an integral part of what the modern, professional officer must become. That is, a professional, knowledgeable, competent, and effective police officer must want to include in his or her body of knowledge about the world an understanding of what ethics means. Everything the officer does hinges on this understanding.

The main focus of this book is in posing the question, "Why should I study ethics?" This is the same as asking, "How can I become a competent officer?"

The point is—embedded in the expectations of police competence is the central, grounding requirement that a police officer have a clear, ethical understanding of the job and possess good moral character. A clear ethic anchors the officer in the good of the community. Without that ethic, the officer is rudderless and lacks personal direction. A police officer's general requirement—like that of other workers—is to do his or her job well. People expect this of each other. But with police officers, invested as they are as the state's instruments of power, the moral and legal ante is raised considerably, and the public expects more. The only thing that both fosters and secures a competent frame of mind in the officer is a dominating interest in doing what is right for the public. It is this, the officer's ethical outlook (revolving around his or her personal character), that over time promotes respect for the police and trust in the police officer. See box I-4.

This book is written to engage the reader in these discussions. We are seeking to treat modern officers as the intelligent and knowledgeable people they are. Instead of talking about "do's" and "don'ts" and attempting to intimidate police officers out of acting inappropriately, we seek to approach the entire subject from the opposite perspective. This work will discuss various schools of ethical thought and their integration with police practice in a way that, as we have said before, works from the ground up. We move from a general understanding toward practical applications. If we succeed, the reader will have a workable and yet theoretically based understanding of ethics that can be applied to the entire gamut of situations police officers encounter on the street every day.

I-3 Organization of the Book

In Part 1 ("The Setting"), we set up several ideas that will echo through the entire book. Chapter 1 ("The New Police Professionalism") makes the case that ethics is a part of the drive to professionalize the police everywhere. Chapter 2 ("Why Be Ethical?") is a discussion of why a person, any

Box I-4

An Ethical Dilemma

Two police officers stop a motorist for speeding. The driver is somewhat cooperative but nevertheless is outraged at the stop and begins to tell the officers that they "should be out catching criminals." Officer A is not particularly upset by this talk, but Officer B is. Officer B bends over to the ground, drops two marijuana joints to the pavement, picks them up, and shows them to the driver saying, "You dropped these." Officer B is now about to arrest the driver for possession of marijuana and take him to jail.

Officer A has seen what has happened and is outraged. But what can Officer A do? What should Officer A do? A concern for duty to the law makes Officer A understand that such behavior on the part of the police is unacceptable. But Officer A also feels another duty—to fellow officers and to the police as a group (to the police subculture).

How can an individual officer resolve such a dilemma between competing duties? Which duty is stronger? What duty does a police officer owe to himself or herself, to the law, and to the police subculture?

person, should consider ethics as an important, integral part of his or her life. It is critical that police officers begin here, and not with police-specific discussions and examples, to better ground their understanding in a framework of thought that is deeper in its significance than an on-the-job type of perspective.

Part 2 ("Ethical Frameworks") develops an understanding of several different schools of thought about ethics. Chapter 3 ("What is Character?") begins our treatment of these schools by discussing the idea of personal character and relating it to police officer ethics. Chapter 4 ("The Development of Character") engages the reader in a consideration of how character is determined and how, even as an adult, the individual officer can work on his or her own character—with an eye toward developing in himself or herself the most competent professional possible.

Chapter 5 ("Ethical Formalism") discusses the idea that there are absolute rules of morality. Developed by the famous philosopher Immanuel Kant, this school of thought suggests that a person's intent, and not the consequences of his or her actions, is all-important in defining right and wrong and in making ethical choices. Chapter 6 ("Utilitarianism") discusses a type of ethical thinking that relies exclusively on calculations of benefit and harm (consequences) brought about

Box I-5

The Book's Central Argument

> Police officers cannot be considered to be competent if they do not underwrite their behavior on the street with a personal ethic that is thoughtfully created and maintained. Ethics and competence are directly linked and inseparable. And they both are largely determined by individual police officer character.

by action. To John Stuart Mill, this school's leading proponent, right and wrong are solely determined by the consequences a person's actions have for the greatest number of people.

Chapter 7 ("An Ethic to Live By") is our attempt to draw the previous chapters together into a concise set of principles that every officer can use as a guide on the street. Chapter 8 ("Judgment Calls") applies this ethic to some of the difficult problems presented to officers on the street. It discusses how a professional, competent officer of good character makes choices between different courses of action.

Part 3 ("Applications") seeks to get the reader even closer to practical applications by relating the theory presented to the world of police work. Chapter 9 ("Types of Police Misconduct") discusses a rather dark side of police work, the various sorts of misbehavior into which officers sometimes fall. Chapter 10 ("Corruption of Authority and Police Crime"), chapter 11 ("Noble Cause Corruption: Confronting Dirty Harry"), and chapter 12 ("Ineptitude and Personal Misconduct") then delve specifically into these different types of misconduct and seek to discuss why and how they should be avoided.

Part 4 ("Implications") attempts to bring the reader back from these discussions of specific types of misconduct to engage the question of how an officer can work on his or her own integrated perspective of police ethics. Chapter 13 ("The Law Enforcement Code of Ethics") argues that the Code of Ethics, despite the criticism that it is unrealistic, is a good frame of reference to use as a basis for understanding ethics on the street. Finally, in Chapter 14 ("On Becoming a Good Officer"), we put everything together, the theory and the practice, the ideal and the real, and reflect on what being a good officer means today and in the future.

Summary

Before we engage our systematic treatment of ethics, a word is in order about the limitations of such an enterprise. First, let us acknowledge the fact that the world is full of good, honest, competent police officers who have never studied ethics. Our endeavor is to enhance the chances that recruits will enter the profession with the ideas and vocabulary of, and sense for reasoning about, ethical matters.

Second, good ethical conduct comes primarily from what a person already has before he or she enrolls in the police academy. It comes from a person's character and upbringing. That is, an "ethically disposed" personality trait is not likely to be created either by simply reading this or any other book or by experiencing training. All we can hope to accomplish in these pages is to enhance the ethical sensibilities of recruits and clarify the absolutely critical relationship between ethics and police competence. See box I-5.

Let us begin by entering into the contemporary debate about what it means to be a professional police officer.

Topics for Discussion

1. The authors suggest that the police give meaning to the law and make it come to life in the daily lives of citizens because of how they (the police) apply it. How is this done? Discuss examples of how the police use their discretionary decision-making powers to "make law" on the street.

2. The law discriminates between people. It treats some people one way and others another. There is nothing wrong with this—in fact, it is the job of the law to do so. Discuss the difference between treating people differently because of their *behavior* (perfectly acceptable) and treating people differently because of their *characteristics* (not ethically defensible).

3. This book attempts to deal with police ethics from what the authors call "a positive" approach. That is, the book spends little time talking about how police officers should avoid being guilty of misconduct and a lot of time talking about police officers having good character. Discuss the difference between "not making mistakes" and "doing the right thing."

The Setting

1

Chapter 1
The New Police
Professionalism

Chapter 2
Why Be Ethical?

In Part 1, we will discuss the importance of ethical judgment for modern-day police professionals, some general thoughts about living a moral life, and the nature of character. To begin with, we must discuss how today's police officers are involved in an exciting set of changes that affect every aspect of their careers. From who is selected to become police officers, to how they are trained, to the level of intellectual sophistication possessed by today's cops on the beat, things are different from what they used to be. It is toward a brief discussion of these dynamic changes and toward an understanding of what the new police professionalism means that we now turn.

1

The New Police Professionalism

> *"Get a haircut. Shine your shoes. Polish your brass. Take some pride in looking professional."*
> —Veteran Sergeant to a Rookie Officer

Outline

There has been a great deal of talk in recent years about something called "police professionalism" as if everyone is certain that he or she knows what is meant by the term. Police administrators, academics who teach college classes in criminal justice, and even politicians consistently call for the professionalization of the police.

Unfortunately, many people, both inside and outside police work, hold a concept of professionalism that is exactly the opposite of what those in the field should be working toward. This is troublesome because for professionalism to develop in American policing, everyone involved must understand the educational, subcultural, and ethical implications of what true professionalism means. Let us begin our discussion of professionalism by reviewing briefly the history of its evolution.

1-1 The History of Police Professionalism

Throughout the history of organized policing, constant reference has been made to the ideal of professionalism. But the definition of professionalism has changed markedly since the beginning of that history (see box 1-1.) We are, therefore, left with a problem when we attempt to understand it. There have been three distinctly different and contradictory definitions for this concept over time. Thus, a debate goes on about what we mean by police professionalism.

When Sir Robert Peel and the English Parliament created the first Anglo-American police force in 1829 (the Metropolitan Police of London), they considered that they had created a "professional" police force because they had replaced a semivoluntary system of night watchmen and constables with an organization that employed people to be police officers on a full-time basis. These people were regarded as professionals because they were hired, trained, and paid to do the job.

However, not everyone who is paid to do a job is a member of a profession. The idea of the professions emerged in the Middle Ages as a byproduct of the development of the university. Initially, professionals included the clergy, lawyers, professors, and physicians. At the time, these groups of people were "educated" in the sense that they all had doctorate degrees. But more than that, they were essentially the only people who could read. With the printing press yet to be invented, professionals were members of a small, elite group of people who had access to books, the world of ideas, and sophisticated learning.

All sorts of people who are not considered professionals do jobs and do them on a full-time basis. They are involved in occupations or careers that do not involve the education, training, experience, responsibilities,

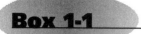

Box 1-1

What Is a Professional?

1. A professional is anyone who does a job for pay (a pro athlete as opposed to an amateur, for example).

2. A professional is anyone who looks clean-cut, disciplined, and polished when on the job (a military standard).

3. A professional is anyone who develops and uses a special skill at work (a carpenter or a plumber, for example).

4. A professional is anyone who possesses an academic experience and possesses a body of knowledge that is unknown to lay people (a physician, lawyer, engineer, or teacher, for example).

and ethical requirements that accompany the true professions. Thus, while people may be butchers, bakers, or candlestick makers and are paid to be such, they are not professionals as are doctors, lawyers, teachers, or engineers.

Generations of police officers have been involved in an occupation that requires hard work, dedication, insight, and courage. Yet, until very recently, police work did not require of them the things that are required of genuine professionals. Making a distinction between the genuine professions on the one hand and occupations on the other is not an exercise in snobbery. As we shall see, this differentiation is critical to the development of an understanding of what modern police officers should be.

Eventually, the first era in the history of policing—the one begun by English statesman Sir Robert Peel and usually referred to as the "Political Era"—was replaced by the "Reform Era." This happened in most places between the 1910 and 1950. During this time frame, to fight the corruption and incompetence that existed in many police circles, strict controls were placed on police officers and police organizations. Chains of command were tightened. Uniforms and a more military look were sharpened up. Internal affairs sections, which investigated accusations of police misconduct, were created. The police academy was invented, and training was taken seriously for the first time. All of this was done in the name of "professionalizing" the police.

So a new, second-generation definition of "professional" was created. With this new definition in mind, people talked of the professional police as a group of newly defined practitioners. This new breed of men (street officers were all men in those days) now had to pass background checks and civil service examinations. They were now sent to training academies, investigated when accused of misconduct, and so on. Police officers began to hear, usually from their sergeants, that they should maintain a professional look and act professionally at all times. At that time, this meant that they should polish their brass, shine their shoes, cut their hair, and behave in a paramilitaristic way.

Part of this era's idea of professionalism was that, like military men, policemen would maintain a civil yet formal and distant relationship with the public. They would never play favorites in the performance of their tasks. They would be objective and legally precise in their application of the law. They would be taught to ignore the lure of payoffs and graft of all sorts and would thus be motivated to do their jobs as honest civil servants. They would be educated about the penal code and case law and would not be ignorant of their roles as legal paraprofessionals. And they would follow the orders that came down from above as if they were in a military organization.

In most places, these changes were effective in doing away with old-style corruption and giving the police a new sense of honor, power, effectiveness, and pride. Yet this second definition of professional was still inappropriate. It focused on the physical appearance of the police officer, on a military model of operations, and on only a part of the knowledge (the law-related part) that the police should possess. It did not take into account the kind of academic experience and behavior that characterizes a true professional.

It has been important to discuss these previous definitions of professionalism because so many people misinterpret the idea today in favor of these out-of-date concepts. But today's police are not professionals merely because they are full-time cops. They also are not professionals merely because they have training, standards of conduct, and uniforms. And they are definitely not professionals because they have chains of command.

Within the last few years, the American police have changed in the direction of becoming genuinely professional in every way. This set of changes, toward a third and more appropriate definition of professionalism, is still under way in some places. It is an exciting and dynamic part of what it means to be a police officer in today's America. And it is toward an understanding of this new, third definition of professionalism that we now turn.

Box 1-2

Several Definitions of "Professional"

Professionals possess:

Knowledge—A systematically organized body of knowledge that lay people (nonprofessionals) do not understand

Education—An academic experience that involves studying and learning this systematically organized body of knowledge within a wider conceptual framework

Regulation—Self-regulation, standards of education and licensing that are set by members of the profession themselves, normally controlled by professional organizations such as the American Medical Association (AMA) or American Bar Association (ABA)

Discipline—Self-policing, investigation, and disciplining of members accused of misconduct by their peer professionals (again, normally done by professional organizations such as the AMA and the ABA)

Problem Solving—Done in a "collegial" manner; all licensed members of the profession are, in a sense, coequal partners in problem solving—using their expertise and insight to solve problems together (rather than operating in an authoritarian, command-driven structure)

1-2 Today's Police Professionalism

Sociologists who study the workplace have a distinct understanding of what separates the professions from what are called "jobs" or "occupations." Box 1-2 provides a summary of the elements that make up the true professions. It makes sense for us here to spend a moment discussing these elements so we will understand the critical nature of how personal ethics fit into the development of police work as a genuine profession.

Today's police officers, as a group, possess some of these characteristics. But because they do not possess them all, the label "professional" is not yet ascribed to the police in the way that it is to others.

1-2a Knowledge

To begin, there is certainly a body of knowledge that must be obtained in high school, college, the police academy, and in-service training experiences to operate as a modern-day police officer. The lay people of the world, even other legal professionals such as lawyers and judges, are not familiar with the complexities of this body of knowledge. Lawyers know case law and codified law; judges also know the law; corrections officers know about dealing with prisoners; psychologists know about adolescent psychology and gang theory; social workers know about ongoing family problems and domestic abuse; criminologists know about the multiple causes of crime; military personnel know about guns and weapons tactics; and medical people know about drug abuse. But no group of people knows as much as an educated police officer does about all of these things at once. One can thus make the argument that the police possess their own distinctive body of knowledge.

1-2b Education

The police are very well trained today. This arguably gives them the type of academic experience that true professionals enjoy. A large number of officers have some college education, and many have earned degrees. Every officer goes to a police academy to obtain specific police-related knowledge. In addition, these academies, which lasted only a few weeks in earlier days, have become fifteen- and twenty-week (or longer) educational experiences.

In most police organizations today, officers are accompanied and trained by field training officers when they first hit the streets. Additionally, in-service training now takes the form of weekly and even daily videotapes, memos from training divisions, and line-up offered discussions about legal and forensic developments in the field of policing. These developments extend the educational and training experience well into the modern officer's career. In fact, the type of life-long learning that is now a part of American police work involves just the type of educational preparation and body of knowledge maintenance that is emblematic of the true profession. Doctors, lawyers, professors, and other professionals are involved in a life-long updating of their knowledge base—and so, too, are today's police officers.

It is clear that today's police possess a systematically organized body of knowledge and an academic experience that is truly professional in its nature. As we shall see, this fact is critical to the modern police officer. We will discuss the sort of personal habits, mental practices, and character traits that a good person and, therefore, a good police officer should cultivate in his or her life. Nothing could be more critical to the development of the good police officer as an individual and to the continuing development of police professionalism as a whole than maintaining a focus on this idea of life-long learning.

Modern police officers must possess, as a personal ethic, an ideal that constantly motivates them to keep in touch with developments in the legal world, in criminology, in forensic science, and so on. The idea that a good, professional officer be both an expert and a continuing student in all of these fields is central. And modern police work, with its support for in-service training and extensive educational experiences, makes this an easily obtainable ideal for the officer who is motivated to be a genuine professional.

1-2c Regulation

With regard to self-regulation, progress in recent years has brought experienced police administrators into positions where they have a great deal to say about hiring practices, testing procedures, and educational/academy standards. For example, states have police officer standards and training (POST) bodies that set standards for police work. These bodies listen to and follow the advice of police administrators. While the type of self-regulation enjoyed by the American Medical Association and the American Bar Association does not yet exist within police work, self-regulation of police is expanding.

Thus, today's police also meet this criterion for professionalism. With regard to our central topic of police ethics, standards for education and training are being set by police leaders as a part of their commitment to the new professionalism we are discussing. The world of police work, in other words, is slowly coming to control (regulate) its own sphere of influence in the name of this new professionalism.

1-2d Discipline

Regarding self-discipline, the story is different. It seems on the surface that the police regulate their own behavior. Except for about thirty jurisdictions wherein civilian review boards handle police discipline, the overwhelming majority of police officers are subject to internal, police-department-operated disciplinary systems. But internal affairs (IA), as it is called almost everywhere, is operated by police administrators and by the city- and county-run institutions that hire and fire the police. IA is not run by police officer organizations. That is to say that police unions and fraternal organizations do not take part in the self-disciplining of the police. In fact, police officer organizations of America often actively fight against IA organizations. When officers are accused of misconduct, it is the police officers' organization (the union) that provides a defense for the accused.

This is not the same as having professional organizations involved in discipline. When doctors or lawyers are accused of misconduct, their professional groups (the doctors' "union," the AMA; or the lawyers' "union," the ABA) have bodies that take an active role in the investigating and disciplining of their own members. Things operate in a similar manner in other professional fields, such as teaching and engineering. However, police officer fraternal organizations have historically been averse to holding misbehaving officers accountable. Consequently, true professional self-disciplining is not yet the standard method of operation in the police work field. The ethical implications of this reality are obvious. For the police to become genuine professionals, they must themselves, as a group, take seriously the disciplining of peers who are guilty of misconduct.

1-2e Problem Solving

The absence of collegial problem solving is also a problem that stands in the way of the development of genuine police professionalism. Chains of command and orders that come down from the top regarding what to do and how to do it present exactly the opposite dynamic to that of the professions. In particular, the changes brought in during the Reform Era, with their paramilitaristic-policing focus, worked against the development of this type of problem solving. Orders come down from the top. Subordinates follow those orders. This is definitely not the model that is followed by professionals in other fields. See box 1-3.

Good news in this area is the development of the idea of community-based policing (CBP). This philosophy empowers individual police officers to make decisions on their own, using their steadily increasing expertise and education levels. Instead of a top-down focus, CBP requires a partnership within police organizations that uses the experience and overall view of middle and upper-level managers in coordination with the day-to-day, on-the-street expertise of the beat cop. When this is done effectively, the combined experience, education, and streetwise knowledge of both groups produce realistic, thoughtful, intelligent solutions to problems on the street.

Box 1-3

Collegial Problem Solving—An Example

Suppose there is a daylight burglary problem in one part of a city. In the days of paramilitary policing, a memorandum might have been generated from somewhere in the middle-management level of the local police department aimed at attacking this problem. A lieutenant or watch commander working within the administration building might very well have put together such a directive, which ordered officers to take certain steps (altering their patrol patterns and so on) to address the burglary problem.

Today, in many community-based-policing- (CBP-) oriented jurisdictions, developing a solution for such a problem would be collegially approached. Middle managers would get together with on-the-street supervisors and the beat officers who patrol the troubled area in an effort to come up with a solution—using everyone's input and expertise. Naturally, the middle managers would contribute a more veteran perspective, having the greatest amount of experience in police work. But the lower-level officers would be given credit for their expertise too.

Beat officers, after all, work on the street, around the clock. They should be familiar not only with the general area's geography but also with the particular burglars who operate in the area, with their cars, and with their habits. Such knowledge should be, and in CBP organizations is, treated with great respect. The solution developed this way would arguably be more logically based and effective than one that, in "the old days," would have come down to the street in a memo written by someone who no longer patrols the beat.

CBP may continue to expand in America, and its idea of using the expertise of lower-level officers—both individually and in groups—as the basis for police decision making may be taken more seriously. If this happens, then one of the roadblocks to police professionalism (that of command-structure-driven paramilitaristic decision making) will be removed. For the purposes of our discussion of police ethics, this is again a critical element.

Empowering street-level officers to make important decisions rather than requiring that they follow commands that come down from above will necessarily involve all police officers using their practical experience and expertise about their beats. But it will also involve the application, on a day-to-day basis, of the individual ethical standards of thousands of police officers in this decision-making process. Thus, as police professionalism expands, driven partly by these dynamics associated with CBP, it will become even more important that individual officers understand and appreciate their police mission in light of their moral views of themselves and of the world.

In section 1-2, "Today's Police Professionalism," we have discussed how the classic sociological definition of professionalism does and does not apply to today's police officers. There is much good news here, and it is with pride that today's officers can look at the dynamic changes that are under way. But to finish our discussion of police professionalism, we must consider how all of this has been put together in a more practical and understandable set of principles. While the characteristics of the profession discussed above are important, they do not tell us much about the actual frame of reference that the professional officer should have as an individual. In section 1-3, "Muir's Passion and Perspective," we will face that idea head on.

1-3 Muir's Passion and Perspective

In one of the most important books ever written about the police (*Police: Streetcorner Politicians,* Chicago, 1977), political science professor and author William K. Muir Jr. discusses police professionalism from a different perspective. He writes that, to operate as true professionals, individual officers must possess "passion and perspective" when applying their considerable expertise to people's real-life problems (see box 1-4).

Let us look at Muir's two ideas and discuss how they create a model for professional policing that is understandable and practical.

1-3a Passion

Muir's first idea is that the professional police officer must possess what he calls the "passion" to use coercive power. By this he means that police officers have to be comfortable using what amounts to extortion to achieve good, desirable ends. Extortion involves obtaining desired behavior from others by using threats to harm something of value to them. Children may be told to behave themselves or they will be spanked. Countries tell one another to behave themselves or they will be invaded. And similarly, police officers will threaten to arrest people unless they do what they are told.

Not all officers are comfortable doing this, however. Some people, and some police officers, are reluctant to threaten others because they feel it

Box 1-4

Muir's Professional Officer

The professional officer possesses:

Passion: The understanding that resorting to violence or threats is ethically acceptable if and only if it is done in the interest of justice and in accordance with the welfare of the community; that no guilt need be associated with the pain or unpleasantness of using force.

Perspective: The development of an inner understanding of the motives of people, a sense of life's causes and effects, and a knowledge of the tragedy of life (that all people suffer sometimes, that everyone yearns for some dignity, and that no individual is worthless).

---

involves bullying people. Not being comfortable with such bullying, many people prefer to use their powers of reason as often as possible to convince people to do the right thing because it is good or just or rational. There is nothing wrong with this idea. In fact, Muir takes great pains to point out that police officers should be experts at controlling behavior in just this way, using logic, intelligence, and their persuasive powers.

But police officers routinely encounter situations where appealing to people's better judgment, logic, religious ethics, or morality does not work. Under these circumstances, Muir writes that the professional officer should not be "conflicted" with reservations about intimidating people. Intimidation, when used as a last resort and in the best interest of justice, is an important tool in the police officer's arsenal of weapons. The use of intimidation must be "integrated," Muir writes, into the daily operating philosophy of the professional officer. If officers are reluctant to use coercive power, they might avoid solving people's problems and thus not get their jobs done.

1-3b Perspective

There is a second characteristic that has to be a part of the professional officer's personal makeup. Muir believes that such officers need to have a certain perspective on life that he calls the "tragic perspective." Suffering from tragedy involves experiencing unfairness, calamity, or disaster. Muir does not suggest that when people suffer in this way their consequently deviant acts should be excused. But he does point out that one key to being a professional is the capacity to understand how tragedy explains a great deal about deviant human behavior.

This involves understanding that misbehavior, deviance, and crime are the products of many different dynamics and situations. Life is full of complex patterns that cause deviance. From this perspective, the professional officer understands that tragic, warping, uncontrollable circumstances, the kind that might affect any of us—cops and civilians alike—sometimes overwhelm people and produce deviance. While people will misbehave and act in ugly and criminal ways at times, there are understandable reasons for such behavior. The intelligent cop must attempt to take these reasons into account. In the eyes of the officer who has this perspective, the circumstances of a person's life will have the effect of mitigating a person's responsibility for deviance.

Muir argues that the modern, professional officer's job involves not merely reacting to crime and violence but understanding the underlying causes for such behavior. While he never implies that the police shouldn't take action when they see crime occurring, he also points out that working for long-term solutions to these problems is the larger role of the professional officer. Especially in an era of community-based policing, the police today are expected to attack enduring problems on their beats and not simply to react in moralistic ways to citizen misconduct when they see it. So Muir's idea here is that the professional is a critical analyst of crime's causes and a student of its various solutions.

But there is more. Because of this tragic reality of life, Muir argues that the world view of the police officer should not divide people into camps, into the "good people" and the "bad people," into "us" and "them." Thinking in this way involves embracing what he calls the "cynical perspective," which suggests that there are different sets of rules for different people: one set for them and another set for us. Muir warns that we should not divide people into "us" and "them" because there is only us— at a certain basic, human level, everyone is of equal value. This is the view of social reality expressed in the tragic perspective.

For the cynical perspective to be applied on the streets by the police, making citizens into the enemy in a real sense, is to create a situation under which the people and the police are mutually suspicious of each other. Any good, competent police officer knows that policing cannot be done effectively without the help of the local community. The cynical perspective works against police-community cooperation and against the development of faith in the police generally.

Summary

Earlier in chapter 1 it was important for us to discuss the history of the development of definitions of professionalism. Everyone in police work needs to know what professionalism is and what it is not. It was then critical for us to consider the sociological definition of professionalism. While progress is being made in that direction, there are roadblocks inhibiting its final development. Both the good news and the bad news need to be analyzed with respect to developments in this area.

Finally, Muir gives us a more practical idea of what it means to be a professional police officer on a minute-to-minute basis. While it is by no means a "how to do it" list of specifics, Muir tells us that the professional officer needs to have integrated into his or her personal character both (1) the passion to use coercive power in the pursuit of just ends and (2) a tragic perspective on life that mitigates against cynicism and jadedness.

One final note is in order about the concept of professionalism. Professionalism is changing the way thousands of police officers view their jobs. The change is from seeing police work as an occupation that gives something to the police officer to seeing police work as a profession to which the police officer owes something. Over time, true professionals are embracing the idea that it is a privilege to be a police officer. This is not just because policing is a good job with great benefits and a dynamic work-a-day experience. It is also because the amount of responsibility and power with which the individual officer is entrusted is unusually great.

In chapter 2, we will discuss the importance of personal ethics that flow from this professionalism. What does it mean to be a good person? What are the habits of character that determine whether we have done good or ill? Chapter 2 explores these and other related questions in an effort to personalize more effectively our discussion of what it means to be an ethical police officer.

Topics for Discussion

1. The text refers to several different, historical definitions of police "professionalism." Why do the authors take time to point out that wearing uniforms, having grooming standards, and operating under chains of command do not make an occupation a "profession"?

2. Applying Muir's tragic perspective, discuss "why there is crime." That is, generate a discussion of the multiple causes of crime that is centered on the idea that tragedy, chance, social circumstances, opportunity, and necessity all drive some people to behave in criminal ways.

3. Discuss the cynical view of the world that suggests that there is a "we" and a "they" that divides people. What would be the consequences if police officers applied one set of rules to those they felt were good people and another set of rules to those they felt were bad people? How would we know which was which? Would we look at ethnic characteristics or religion or gender? What's wrong with doing this?

Why Be Ethical?

2

> "If we live from day to day without self-examination, we remain unaware of the dangers we may pose to ourselves and the world."
> — Wallace Shawn, *Aunt Dan and Lemon* (New York, 1991)

Outline

Why should a person be concerned with ethics? What is so important about doing the right thing? Isn't the world full of people who bend the rules, cheat the edges, and work the system in their favor? Don't we worship achievement so much that at times it seems it doesn't matter how you played the game, it only matters whether you won or lost? A survey of Americans once found that a majority would take an illegal drug if they thought it would guarantee they would win an Olympic medal. In such an ends-oriented society, why bother trying to be ethical, moral, and right?

There are many answers to this question, and some of them make up part of the ethical frames of reference that we will discuss later in this chapter. Box 2-1 indicates several different reasons for being concerned about ethics. But in the grand scheme of things, there is an overarching reason that all people should be concerned with values, norms of conduct, ethics, morals, and character. These are the very things that make us humans. In other words, at the most basic level, to be concerned about ethics is to be a human being.

2-1 Ethics Make Us Human

What differentiates humans from other members of the animal kingdom? We are animals, of course, mammals in fact, who have all of the basic needs that other animals possess. We need water, food, rest, and warmth (clothing and shelter) to survive on a daily basis. And so we have the same drives to obtain these things as do the animals. Furthermore, like the animals, we need to procreate. So we also have sex drives that are animalistic in their basic nature.

But what makes us people is our sense of self and of morality. We are the only species that can think in abstract ways, read, write and build inventions out of our own creativity. And in putting together what we call "society," we are the only species that has created rules of conduct, norms, laws, and morals that require each of us to (at times) overcome our animal instincts and control ourselves in ways that are in a real sense "not natural." We are thus the only animals that put together codes of conduct that seek to control our animalistic or hedonistic impulses. Civilization is all about these rules and this attempt to discipline ourselves.

For example, humans created the institution of marriage to organize society in a way that is (or at least historically seemed to be) best suited to

Box 2-1

Why Be Ethical?

Our study will consider several different perspectives on ethical thought, each of which has a somewhat different answer to this question.

Perspective	Answer
Ethical Formalism:	The world works better this way; it's rational to do one's duty and follow principles.
Utilitarianism:	It is better for everyone, including the individual, to do what benefits the majority.
Religion:	We must be ethical because God commands that we be so.

raising children and to maintaining the long-term social order. It takes longer to "raise" human children than it does to raise offspring of virtually any other species. To ensure parents are committed to their young for this extended period of time (about eighteen years or so) and thus ensure that human children learn all they need to know to reach the independence and maturity of adulthood, marriage requires a certain long-term commitment. It requires sexual fidelity, financial responsibility, legal obligations to support children, and so on. It requires sacrifices. For example, married couples must eschew the natural desire to have sex whenever and with whomever they wish.

This is just one example of how we use our rational minds to decide upon norms of conduct, upon rules and obligations that maintain order, and even upon codified laws. These norms, rules, and laws are supposed to be in the best interest of society.

So our norms, rules, and laws—our ethics—are what make us different from all other species. The job of our social institutions—families, schools, religions, economic systems, laws, and so forth—is to instill these principals in people and maintain adherence to them. The job of police officers, among others, is to apply such norms, rules, and laws in a way that encourages order and civility among people.

While it is obviously important for all people to concern themselves with ethics, it is of absolutely critical importance that police officers do so.

Anyone who wishes to be a police officer but who thinks that such concerns about ethics are irrelevant to his or her job has misunderstood what it is that police do. Such an individual is not a good candidate to be a police officer as he or she doesn't possess the most basic understanding of what makes us human and what police are supposed to be doing on the street.

As we will see in Part 2, and as is briefly indicated in box 2-1, the reasons for being ethical have been further divided by analysts and philosophers into several sets of ideas, each with a different perspective. (We, too, will develop our own, separate ethical perspective in chapter 7.) These perspectives all include as their most basic principle this idea that ethics are the central thing that makes us human.

Thus, to the followers of Ethical Formalism (Immanual Kant's philosophy, chapter 5), being ethical is something that everyone should do because it is logical and rational to do so. Human beings owe a duty to society, to each other, and to themselves to be ethical as part of the requirement to behave as rational beings.

From a different perspective, utilitarians (John Stuart Mill's philosophy, chapter 6) believe that being ethical, as they define it, is something that people ought to do because it involves behaving in the interests of the majority of society's members. Utilitarian principles also suggest that behaving ethically involves caring for and nurturing others, a natural drive that helps (again) society to proceed in the most fair and equitable manner.

Religion takes the approach that ethics come from a higher source, from a supreme being or authority (God). But religion is similar to these other schools in that it clearly prescribes the idea that behaving in an ethical manner is critical to one's humanity. Again, ethics differentiate humans from the "beasts."

While these perspectives take different views of ethics and give us different general guidelines for approaching ethical dilemmas, they all focus on the critical importance of ethical behavior in the lives of all intelligent and civilized people.

2-2 Police Moralizing

Our discussion thus far has pointed out why it is important for all people to be ethical and why ethics are an important component of the drive to professionalize the police. But it is critical at this point for us to engage in a discussion of the practical reasons why police officers are particularly prone to be confronted with ethical questions and dilemmas in their professional lives. The reasons are several.

First, police work is all about making critical decisions about other people's lives. The discretionary decision-making power the law gives to the police involves deciding when to make (and when not to make) arrests. It involves when to use (and when not to use) force. It involves what level of force to use in dealing with deviant citizens. In making decisions about arrest and force in particular, the individual police officer makes decisions that affect people's lives profoundly. These are life-changing and, on occasion, life-threatening decisions.

Such decisions must be made in a logical, intelligent, educated manner with an eye toward what is in the best interests of justice. And in focusing on the ideal of justice, each officer must consider what justice means for the individual citizen, for other closely related citizens, and for society in general. So, to begin with, the police make discretionary decisions that must take into consideration the meaning of justice, of community, and of morality.

For example, the individual police officer is empowered to treat a shoplifter in several very different ways. A first-time shoplifter with no record of criminal behavior may be given a warning or lecture or, in the case of a child, may be taken home to Mom and Dad to be dealt with by the institution of the family. On the other hand, a shoplifter may be cited or arrested and taken to jail or juvenile hall. The decision with respect to such minor offenses is clearly left in the hands of the police.

What will they do, what should they do, in the interest of justice? The answer is that "it depends." It depends on the circumstances, what was stolen, the attitude of the suspect, the attitude of parents, the (perceived) interests of the shop owner, and so on. The criminal justice system not only wants, it also expects the police to use their judgment in such cases, and it is totally appropriate that it does so. As the California Penal Code section in box 2-2 indicates, the police are not supposed to apply the law arbitrarily but with "an eye toward justice."

Second, police officers are often faced with conflicting interests. On a regular basis, the cop on the beat must judge the relative merits of conflicting claims from citizens with different perspectives. This is even more difficult than simply exercising the discretionary decision-making power discussed above because quite often both parties in a dispute have legitimate claims. Thus, the individual officer on the street is often presented with two (or even more) sides to a story that are correct from the perspectives of the citizens involved.

Box 2-2

California Penal Code, Preliminary Provisions, Section 4

The rule of the Common Law that penal statues are to be strictly construed
has no application to this code. All of its provisions are to be construed
according to the fair import of their terms with view to affect its objects
and to promote justice.

For example, what should police officers do about a Saturday night
complaint regarding a loud party in a college town? Certainly the peace
and quiet of any neighborhood should be respected. And people must be
listened to when they wish to be protected from what they consider
obnoxious music. Yet partygoers, especially on a Saturday night, have their
rights too. If not on a Saturday night after a victorious football game,
when can a large group of people have a party? What about the rights of
150 people to celebrate their football team's victory?

Again, the answer to the question, "What should the police do?" about
such a complaint is, "It depends." It depends on how late at night it is, how
many people are partying, how many complainants there are, how often
this has been a problem in the past, and so on. There is no "how to do it"
manual for deciding among such legitimate claims between citizens who
each want the law to respond to their legitimate demands.

Sometimes in police work such balancing of interests is not required.
It is clear that an arrest for a violent, felonious crime (armed robbery, for
example) should be made irrespective of what anyone in a neighborhood
believes should be done. Under such circumstances, the duty of the police
to the people is clear. If the elements of the crime are present and there is
probable cause to believe that a suspect is responsible, then the arrest for
a violent felony should be made.

But such incidents are rare in police work. For as much as police officers, inexperienced police officers in particular, focus on dealing with violent felonies as a central part of the law enforcement role they perform,
such arrests make up only a small part of what the police do on a day-to-
day basis. Any number of studies indicates that 90 percent of what the
police do is service and order-maintenance oriented. (See, for example,
James Q. Wilson's *Varieties of Police Behavior,* Cambridge, 1968.) Thus,
more often than not, the police are handling the sort of minor details discussed in the loud party example. Calls about quarreling lovers, loud par-

ties, drunks in a bar, juveniles on a street corner, homeless people in business districts, and so on make up the overwhelming majority of police calls. And in all of these commonplace examples, the police are required to face ethical dilemmas and conflicting claims and make moral judgments about people and events.

Thus, the police are forever moralizing for others. And in doing so, they must make decisions based on what? The answer is that they make decisions based on their own ethics and view of justice in the world—based on their character. Thus, it is unavoidable that the police, more than average citizens, be in close contact with solidly based, well-thought-out sets of ethical principles.

2-3 The Use of Power

It is often said that the police are very powerful individuals. When we hear this, we tend to focus on the fact that the police are licensed to use force on citizens in a way that no other agents of the state are. Yet it is important to acknowledge that there are different ways to do the job of controlling people's behavior. Power is the ability to exercise control over others. And there are three different types of power the police can use. See box 2-3.

Because the power of the police to use force is so apparent, and because people so often object to this type of power, most people focus on coercive power as *the* way that police obtain cooperation from citizens. Any time police are nearby, the implied threat of arrest is present. The uniforms, badges, weapons, and carriage of the police also imply that they are ready to use violence. None of these threats is unrealistic. They are substantial.

But focusing on police power as exclusively relating to the use of violence suggests that threats to arrest or use force are the only means at the disposal of the police, that these are the only tools the police use in controlling people's behavior. Nothing could be further from the truth. The police can also use their powers of logic and intellectual persuasion to convince people to behave themselves (using exhortative power) or they can exchange something to obtain desired behavior (using reciprocal power).

Consider the following examples. Because of their authority, intelligence, and civility, the police regularly convince people to behave themselves using exhortative power. Police officers convince drunks to go home and sleep it off. They convince teenagers to "straighten up and fly

Box 2-3

The Three Types of Power

Exhortation: Convincing people, through the appeal to logic or reason or morals, to do the "right" thing, the "logical" thing, the "honest" thing, the "moral" thing.

Reciprocity: Exchanging something to obtain the desired behavior from another.

Coercion: Obtaining desired behavior using threats to harm something of value to the person being coerced.

right." They convince quarreling spouses to calm down in the interest of their children. They convince teenagers not to join gangs. In these and a hundred other ways, the police use their powers of persuasion to accomplish the job of controlling people's behavior.

Similarly, the police use reciprocal power (exchange) on many occasions. They obtain cooperation by promising to look into the arrest of a friend or relative. They obtain information by going easy on someone. They handle a detail involving homeless people by getting them to a shelter and so on. In this way, the police exchange something of value with citizens to obtain what they (the police) want.

Coercive power is also available, but the intelligent, professional police officer uses it only as a last resort. That is, instead of threatening people, the officer tries the other forms of behavior control first. If it is at all possible, the police use their authority, education, training, substantial resources, good will, and moral standing either in exchange for desired behavior or to convince people how to behave.

When the police use these other forms of power, they are most effective in doing their jobs because people do not react to exhortation and reciprocity the way they do to coercion. Coercion sets up an animosity toward the police that can come back to haunt officers in the future. See box 2-4.

Of course, it is not always possible to go the easier route and use the two more gentle types of persuasion. When that is the case, police officers, as Muir tells us, must feel perfectly at home with coercing people. But the point cannot be emphasized too often that coercion should be the last resort when attempting to control people. As the educated, well-trained, intelligent people that they are, the modern police must always attempt to

Box 2-4

Avoiding the Use of Coercive Power

At the Berkeley Police Department in the 1980s, officers were consistently frustrated by attempting to control homeless people using only coercive power ("move along or you'll go to jail"). Berkeley had an extremely large homeless population, and the limitations of threatening people on a regular basis were made apparent daily. The people didn't like being coerced, and the police didn't particularly like to do it.

In cooperation with several local businesses, the police developed a program wherein people could be given coupons by the police. These coupons were redeemable for free coffee, for example, at several local stores. When the police wanted to achieve some level of cooperation from homeless people in particular, such coupons could be given to cooperating citizens in "exchange" or as a reward for behaving themselves.

Citizens, and the police too, felt better about such an exchange-related type of interaction than they did about being coerced or using coercion. In this way, coercive power was changed into reciprocal power.

exhort people to do the right thing. When they can accomplish this, the police have operated effectively and have left people with the feeling that they did the right thing on their own. This makes people feel good about themselves and (even) about the police. Such positive feelings reap rewards in the future in terms of citizen-police cooperation that benefits everyone: the beat officer, the detective, the individual citizen, and the community.

2-4 Character As a Focal Point

We have pointed out that the police have a great deal of discretionary power. It should be obvious from the discussion in section 2-3, "The Use of Power," that when decisions are made to arrest or not to arrest, to use force or not to use force, or to use various levels of force, the police are operating in the area of coercive power. While this is an important part of police work and this power is an important power in the arsenal of the individual officer, it should be clear that the police make another type of decision on a regular basis. They decide what type of power to exercise over citizens. We have argued here that the professional officer should use exhortative and reciprocal power as often as is practical.

There is an ethical component to each of these types of decisions. The character of individual police officers is of critical importance, for example, when attempting to control people. The competent, professional officer will avoid using coercive power whenever possible, even though in the police world there is a great deal of romantic, macho-driven support for acting like a "cowboy." It might seem like fun and feel like a more appropriate method of operation (given police norms regarding toughness), but coercing people has long-term drawbacks that need to be avoided if possible. The officer who possesses a well understood ethical frame of reference will understand this and will take the less troublesome routes to obtaining citizen cooperation. But it takes strength of will and character to do so.

Sometimes there is confusion regarding how to make judgments on the street—regarding what considerations to take into account. As we shall see in Part 2, such decisions can be made based on different ethical grounds depending on the circumstances of a given detail. Sometimes, absolute principles seem to be called for. An arrest for a violent felony must be made irrespective of circumstances and the identities of participants. This type of ethical decision making is called Ethical Formalism (see chapter 5).

At other times, circumstances such as the age of citizens, the location of events, the intentions of suspects, the previous records of those involved, and so on will play a major role in arrest decisions. When making calculations that relate to the greater good of the community regarding minor crimes, for example, police officers use a less absolutist and more relativistic set of principles. This type of ethics is called utilitarianism (see chapter 6).

When attempting to use non-coercive power to obtain their desired ends, the police are using utilitarianism. They are treating different situations in different ways, taking into account the good of the community and the interests of individual citizens. When the police give citizens the chance to decide to do the right thing for themselves, in other words, they are acting in an utilitarian manner.

When and how these different perspectives should be used is often not clear, and that is why we have created our "ethic to live by" for police officers (see chapter 7). But it is clear that with so many diverse roles to play, with so many conflicting demands being made by citizens, with so many types of crimes to consider and options available to them, the police are confronted with a confusing reality. And rather than try to sort this reality out in a piecemeal way, our effort here will attempt to focus on one central idea that links all ethical schools of thought together, that of police officer character.

Summary

In chapter 2, we have considered the importance of ethics in the lives of all human beings, the nature of the moralizing that police in particular must do every day, the nature of the power that they possess, and the importance of understanding various types of behavior control. In doing so, we have outlined the importance of living an ethical life and the critical nature of the ethical foundation upon which police officer decision making must rest.

In chapter 3, we will consider the personal character dynamics involved in attempting to accomplish these tasks. As we have taken some trouble to point out in chapter 2, the personal ethics of individual police officers are critical to the impact the entire criminal justice system has on life on the street. And within individual officers themselves, the character they possess forms the basis for the application of ethics to the everyday problems of people in America.

Topics for Discussion

1. Discuss why "ethics make us human." Why do philosophers and religious authorities agree that the single most important difference between the animal kingdom and human beings is this propensity to create moral codes and control natural instincts?
2. The authors suggest that police officers are regularly confronted with details wherein "both sides are right." Discuss examples of confrontations where the police have to "referee" between citizens (or groups of citizens), each of whom is, from his or her perspective, right.
3. Discuss examples of the three types of power. Use non-police examples first and then move to consider some police-related uses of exhortative, reciprocal, and coercive power.

Part

Ethical Frameworks

2

The ethical theory that we develop here—"an ethic to live by"—is a hybrid or combination built out of certain aspects of Immanuel Kant's theory of duty and John Stuart Mill's idea of utility. Our account differs from those of these two philosophers chiefly in the importance we give to the idea of character. While theirs are principle-based ethics, ours is character-based. For them, the first question that is most relevant to ethics is, "What ethical principle applies to this situation?" For us, the first question is, "What kind of person do I want to be?"

For Kant and Mill, ethical discussions begin with the problem of making specific choices; for us, to begin with decision-making rules assumes too much. For them, ethics is largely a matter of rules while for us it is a matter of how to live. In Part 2, we will present our "ethic to live by" for the police officer, building it upon a two-chapter discussion about the nature of character, what it is, how we get it, and how it operates, and then upon the ideas discussed by Kant and Mill. We begin by discussing character and why it is so critical to police officers and to the delivery of justice on the streets.

Chapter 3
Personality: Extrovert, nice, Moody

Character:
Core
Conscious

2 forces that drives humans: (Freud)
Sex: (reproduction)

Death: (Avoidance) ↳ self-destruction)
↓
survival

Things we do, decision, and motivation is combined by sex + Death.
fear of falling + Loud noises

[handwritten top notes:]

D: primitive, instant gratification. Bad thoughts, lack of morals and values and Darkest thought that are not socially accepted.
EGO-Balance, Concious, Mediator and every day person that balance I D and superego. (self I mpr is out of balance)

uperego: pleasure, tempts death, thrill seeking (Dreams / safe)

ncept of flight | or fight (Angel)

[handwritten:]
D + SuperEgo are unconcious
go is concious

What Is Character?

[handwritten:]
uperego rest off of sleep
Rapid eye is the deepest sleep

> *"Character is what you do when nobody's looking."*
> — Anonymous

Outline

[handwritten:]
Character is what you do alone. Not how someone sees you.

Personality is how others see you.

Freud is from Austria

Over active I D and Superego or a break down of your Ego is how psychos define rime.

Character is one of those elements of life that is assumed to be understood by everyone. Yet few people have ever thought much about its definition. For example, elections are driven by debates about the good or bad character of candidates for office. But when we analyze such political discussions, we find that the term "character" has no specific substance to it other than this: Politicians have good character if we support them, they lack character if we do not.

Character in the competent police officer is so important that we cannot proceed in this work without a solidly constructed definition. We need to have a good grasp of character here because our central thesis is that character is the single most important determiner of police officer competence and effectiveness. Character is not just a part of what makes up police professionalism; it is the essential element in professionalism. See box 3-1.

3-1 Character and Virtue

In seeking to understand character, we must engage in an ancient debate about whether character determines behavior or behavior determines character. This chicken-or-egg argument is basic to understanding the concept.

It seems axiomatic to many people that a person's character is defined by his or her actions. In fact, this school of thought suggests that what one thinks, believes, and says is largely window dressing in life. Thoughts, beliefs, and talk are all irrelevant to who a person really is. The only thing that counts is what a person does. If a person knows the right thing to do in a given situation, for example, but fails to do it, then he or she has shown poor character.

If a person behaves, on a regular basis, in a way that is despicable, certainly no one would suggest that person "has good character on the inside but behaves abominably on the outside." Few would accept the idea that the person's misconduct was irrelevant to an analysis of his or her character. To take an extreme example, it seems absurd to suggest that someone who helped to operate the gas chambers of the Holocaust was somehow, deep inside, a good person.

Nevertheless, there is a school of thought (the other side of this argument) that suggests good character is largely determined independently of action. Aristotle is the premiere philosopher here. His idea was that people who wish to live good lives should seek to live like moral heroes (*Nicomachean Ethics*). Aristotle talked of attempting to behave like "exemplars" or "role models," as we might say today. This school of thought focuses on the idea of virtue (today, we often label this school "the ethics of virtue") as being the most important focal point when discussing ethics. In ancient times, Plato discussed the "just person" in all his dialogues; Aristotle focused on the "person of moral wisdom" in his

Box 3-1

Two Different Views of Character

In the debate about the nature of character, one side suggests that character is hard to fathom, a difficult-to-understand quality that is hidden deep within the individual. This view suggests that character is independent of action. Thus:

"We cannot judge ... the character of men with perfect accuracy, from their actions or their appearance in public; it is from their careless conversation, their half-finished sentences, that we may hope with the greatest probability of success to discover their real character."

— Maria Edgeworth
(Irish Novelist)

But others believe that the character of people, who they really are and what they stand for, is completely determined by their behavior. What people say they will do or believe they will do is irrelevant. All that matters is their actions. Thus:

"What is character but the determination of incident? What is incident but the illustration of character?"

— Henry James
(American Novelist)

Nicomachean Ethics; and in his *City of God,* St. Augustine discussed the "citizen of the city of God." These concepts each encompass the same idea: To believe in virtuous principles and to attempt to live a good life is enough. A person of good character cultivates these ideals and attempts to acknowledge them in his or her life's works.

Religious heroes can be relevant to this school of thought too. To attempt to live like Jesus, Confucius, Buddha, or Mohammed is the point of the ethics of virtue. If you organize your life in a way such that this is the goal, then you are leading a good life. In other words, if you attempt to live such a life, you are a good person—even if you fail in your actions to do so.

Thus, the ethics of virtue do not focus on absolute rules of conduct applicable to everyone at all times but rather on the internalized character of the individual. This school of thought suggests that the individual of good character might behave in different ways at different times given different circumstances and different goals. Times change; people change; different people need and want different things; and no two situations are ever exactly the same.

Suppose that a police officer has a music store on his or her beat and is regularly presented with details where sales personnel have detained shoplifters. On one Christmas week workday, the officer is confronted with three such details. In one instance, the suspect is a 17-year-old gang member who has stolen some CDs to sell for cash. In another instance, the suspect is a 15-year-old welfare recipient who has stolen several CDs to give as Christmas presents. In still another instance, an upper-middle-class 16-year-old has stolen CDs for her own personal use.

The gang member, who has a long record of arrests, "knows the drill" and is reasonably cooperative and deferential to the police officer. The welfare recipient, who has no record whatsoever, is visibly upset. She is not only scared about being caught, but she is obviously embarrassed that due to her financial situation she is stealing Christmas presents. The upper-middle-class teenager is belligerent, telling the police officer that she is not a common criminal, is a very important person, and should not be "harassed" by the police.

What should the officer do? Several schools of ethical thought that believe in absolute rules of conduct (see chapter 5) would say that, in the interests of equality, each of these suspects should be treated in exactly the same way. This is what the rule of law demands. To approach similar details in different ways, taking into consideration the individual circumstances, would be to ignore the requirement that the law be absolute in its application. Furthermore, to treat people differently due to their status and histories would be to ignore one of the principles of law: that the police officer is an agent of the state who merely applies the dictates of the law in an evenhanded manner on the street. Equality of treatment, and only equality of treatment, is important from such an absolutist perspective. Thus, arresting all three suspects and taking them all to jail would be the ethical thing to do.

The ethics of virtue, however, might suggest otherwise. The virtuous officer would have the greater, long-term interests of justice in mind. And what is just can be different from what is equal. The virtuous police officer would focus on the long-term implications—for the community, for the music store, and for the individual suspects—of taking different types of action. It might be in the interests of justice and crime control to (1) arrest the gang member and deal with him firmly, (2) issue a stern warning to the welfare recipient and release her, and (3) take the upper-middle-class suspect home to her parents and explain the situation.

Each of these solutions is appropriately aimed at the accomplishment of the officer's duties to victims, suspects, and community. Yet each situation has been dealt with in a different, unequal way. The ethics of virtue, driven by the good character of the police officer, would accept these inequities and rationalize that there really wasn't any different treatment involved. The police officer was always acting in the best interest of each suspect and always in the best interest of the community. Justice and crime control (in the long run) were always the focus of these different actions. And thus, in treating each instance differently, the officer was doing the ethical and virtuous thing.

Aristotle came to define virtue as what he called the Golden Mean (*Nicomachean Ethics*). Simply stated, this concept suggests that circumstances in life tend to trigger a natural range of response, and this range includes a mean between excessive and defective responses (see table 3-1). These habitual or accustomed ways of responding are a person's "character traits." The individuals who are the most admirable are those who habitually or "characteristically" find the norm between these two extremes.

For example, Aristotle argued that one indication of a person's character was how he or she dealt with money. If people were too possessive of their money, they would be guilty of stinginess. If they were too free with it, willing to give money away, they would be guilty of extravagance. The Golden Mean lies in between. It terms of dealing with money, it is generosity. Being generous is one of the elements of having good character.

Some examples of personal defects, according to Aristotle, include cowardice, insensitivity, stinginess, small-mindedness, apathy, self-deprecation, and shamelessness. Excesses include recklessness, self-indulgence, extravagance, having a short temper, vanity, boastfulness, and being terror-stricken. The virtues include courage, self-control, generosity, high-mindedness, gentleness, truthfulness, and modesty. More than two thousand years after it was created, Aristotle's list still makes a good menu of virtues. How could anyone argue with the assertion that a person who possessed these traits would be a person of good character?

This specific discussion of Aristotle's virtues will now be developed into a more general explanation of the elements of character as they have come to be defined through the ages. What makes up character? What are its elements?

TABLE **3-1**   Aristotle's Virtues

Area	Defect	Mean	Excess
fear	cowardice	courage	recklessness
pleasure	insensitivity	self-control	self-indulgence
money	stinginess	generosity	extravagance
honor	small-mindedness	high-mindedness	vanity
anger	apathy	gentleness	short temper
truth	self-depreciation	truthfulness	boastfulness
shame	shamelessness	modesty	terror-stricken

3-2 Moral Judgment

Character must be differentiated from personality. Personality consists of the "outermost" indicators of an individual's makeup, those traits such as intelligence, wittiness, or charm that make an impression on others. Character, on the other hand, refers to one's "inner" makeup, those traits that indicate the person's habitual moral qualities or defects (the composite of virtues and vices). When we ask if people have good character, we are asking if they are honest, if they possess the moral strength to do the right thing, if they are courageous, if they have a solid understanding of what constitutes the good in life, and if they possess integrity.

Integrity is a part of good character that is of particular importance in police officers. Integrity is that characteristic of wholeness, unity, and completeness that means a person is well rounded in his or her approach to life. It is critical that police officers have integrity because they must possess multiple sets of skills, areas of substantive knowledge, practical understandings of the real world, and physical/athletic abilities. Ethics and integrity thus play off of each other in a mutually dependent way. To draw together all the characteristics, knowledge, and skills that are necessary to make up a competent, professional police officer, one needs the interweaving "glue" of an ethical perspective. An intelligent and thoughtfully developed ethical perspective is essential to personal integrity. And integrity is a key ingredient in good character.

Good character, then, is absolutely essential to the development of police professionalism. This may seem to be a simple truism. But we mean to say much more than "good character is a good thing for a police officer to possess." Our thesis is that without a consciously thought-out commitment to living an ethical professional life, without good character, no amount of intelligence, training, skill, or physical ability will suffice. Put more bluntly, you cannot be a good police officer without having good character. All of the rest is wasted if officers do not underwrite their traits, skills, and experiences with an understanding of the ethical implications of life.

We now turn to a consideration of the elements of character that will make more clear what it is and why it is so critical.

3-2a Judgments About Possibilities

The dominating, central fact about the intelligence of human life is that it is so open to possibility. Unlike animals, we see our lives reflectively. That is, we see our lives in terms of our memories and imagination, in terms of our plans, beliefs, and ideas. We daydream, we wonder, we plan, we fantasize, we assess possibilities, and we live accordingly.

Animals adapt to their environments in a way that makes them part of it. The gazelle, for example, is exquisitely matched to its surroundings, but its lovely leap will never take it outside the savanna. The biology of adaptation fixes the life of the animal through its instincts, and no other options are available to it. Human beings adapt to their surroundings, too, but by reflection, not biology. Unlike animals, people can live anywhere because they can change their environments to suit their needs—by cutting trees, irrigating fields, farming, or domesticating animals. Then, too, people can change themselves to suit the environment—for example, by making clothing, wearing scuba gear, innoculating themselves against disease, physical training.

A person's options are not determined in advance by the laws of nature. Instead, they are indeterminate. Only a person's imagination limits the range of options. The conduct of a person's life has all the characteristics of an unfolding plan. And our personal past histories are parts of that plan. See box 3-2.

Our histories can be seen as including two sets of constantly converging possibilities: (1) those things which might or might not have happened to us (fate), and (2) those things which we might or might not have done (our choices). On looking back at our lives, we may regret what might have been, seeing other possibilities for ourselves and regretting the sudden turns of fortune. Or we might equally regret choices we made, reflecting upon the other possible lives we might have made for ourselves. Or we may feel we were lucky things turned out as they did and that if we had it to do over again, we would do the same things.

Box 3-2

The Two Impacts of "Possibilities" on Our Lives

1. **Fate:** Possible outcomes that happen to us
2. **Choice:** Possible outcomes that we control

In this self-reflection, we make moral judgments of different kinds about the past. People might think that they ought to have chosen differently at various junctures (to marry or not to marry, to have children or not to have children, to pursue careers that involved doing work important to them or to pursue careers aimed at getting a lot of money, and so on). In such moral reflection, we are aware of our present desires and feelings and our present situations, and we link those to past good and bad fortune and good and bad choices.

We explain ourselves to ourselves in terms of our own history. Our recollections, however, are always colored with a sense of unrealized possibilities, by the things that might have been. And the things that *could* have happened are crucial parts of our lives. Our personal histories are thus filled with a sense of *what if* and *what I should have done.* Thus, our nature, the quality of our lives, and our character do not merely depend on events and actions that did occur, but also on possibilities, real possibilities, that we did not act upon, for one reason or another. This consideration of possibility may be pushed very far, and it is the essence of moral reflection.

Moral judgments, that is, judgments about right and wrong, about good and evil, are best understood as a class of judgments about possibilities. The natural setting of such judgments is within personal deliberation where, either publicly or in the privacy of our own minds, we compare and evaluate possibilities. This deliberation happens in families, in offices, on job sites, or wherever people meet to discuss or argue about how to get along. We talk, we think, we listen, we respond, and together with those around us, we develop our understandings of ourselves, of the world, and of morality. At the interpersonal level, this is the way people create, maintain, and change the norms and values of entire cultures.

But people are not all the same. They have different points of view. This variation in points of view is the natural consequence of the fact that people do not live the same lives. When people are well matched, when they have a lot in common, their points of view will overlap. In the case of good friends or lovers, their views will quite often reflect each other's, depending on how long they have been together. Their two lives blend together because they have come to share similar values and, to some extent, they have each influenced the tolerances and expectations of the other. There remains, however, a difference between them, and they depend on it. They know themselves and each other by this difference. They enjoy and rely on each other because of the common place they have come to inhabit from the different courses of their two lives.

Thus, even in the case of close friends with "a lot in common," we have different perspectives because of our different histories. We have experienced different possibilities, both in the sense that fate has presented us all with different experiences and in the sense that we have made different choices between possibilities. Differences present both the interesting commonalties that make for friendship, issues to which we must make adjustment, and areas wherein we must find ways to get along. They produce both the comfort of agreement and the predicament of disagreement. From this basic fact comes the core notion of procedural justice—that there are "rules of the game" for getting along and for deciding differences. See box 3-3.

3-2b Justice

In our discussion of ethics, we will consider justice to be the requirement for fairness. It is a moral concept. It may be the most elementary and most prevalent moral aspect of how people get along with each other as well as the condition for the development of most other moral concepts. The concept of justice emerges from the common type of human interaction that is found everywhere. Justice is essential to the possibility of satisfactory relationships and to the possibility of the development of community between people.

The community into which children are born is a major shaping force in their lives. The language and religion of their people, the emotions of their family, the way they are cared for, what they learn to expect, the norms and values created and maintained by society's major institutions—children begin to assimilate all of this long before acquiring a clear sense of their independence and individuality. They are thus socialized from the earliest of their experiences and continually throughout their lives.

The child's original community, his or her family, provides the conditions for the development of his or her mental and social abilities. It is

Box 3-3

Learning About Truthfulness and "Lying"

Is it wrong to tell a lie? Some would make this an absolute rule of life—a moral principle that should always govern interpersonal relationships. Others might say, "It depends." It might be acceptable to lie under certain circumstances and not under others.

For example, is it immoral to tell children "lies" about Santa Claus, the Easter Bunny, and the Tooth Fairy? When filling stockings in the middle of the night or hiding Easter eggs or taking a tooth from under a pillow, parents are, in fact, deceiving their children—lying to them. No amount of "little white lie" rationalizations can change this reality. The question is, of course, is this kind of lie somehow acceptable because no harm is meant by it? It is, in fact, the product of parental love in a sense.

Now in most families that play the Santa Claus game, for example, an interesting twist is made when older children grow out of believing in this myth. They, the older children, begin to help Mom and Dad "be Santa" by filling stockings and so on for those younger siblings who are still believers. Here is a good example of how children, in the home, learn the rules of interpersonal relationships—that telling such little white lies is not only acceptable, but it also helps to create an atmosphere of excitement and wonder around holiday time. It is not really lying, they learn, to talk of Santa Claus and reindeer and so on.

---

the original source of the development of the sense of individuality, of self. And the nature of this original community builds in a demand for some form of justice, that is, for fair treatment, for the chance to be taken seriously and to count in the estimation of others. Children will protest if they aren't given the same treatment as their brothers and sisters, whether it be in terms of food, clothing, and love; in terms of discipline; or even in terms of gifts at holiday time. Children will (naturally) protest if they are not listened to, if their ideas are not taken seriously, and so on. The voice of this protest is the voice that demands justice.

This natural demand for justice creates in children a sense of how relationships with other people, both friends and family, work—the rules of the relationship game. In learning what is and is not appropriate in relationships, they engage certain virtues such as truthfulness, kindness, trustworthiness, and loyalty, the basic qualities essential to a common life. They, therefore, learn how to care for others and for themselves.

We all bring this sense of justice with us into adult life. It is an underlying theme of all morality. Dealing with people justly and fairly is necessary to keeping a balance between different ideas of what is good (differing views of life's possibilities) and to support procedures for deciding differences. Put another way, at the core of public morality is a concern for how people ought to interact, ought to get along, ought to argue (when they argue), and ought to solve problems when disagreements arise. Without agreement upon how this process (for deciding differences) works, any society would be in chaos.

Much of what police officers do deals with people in conflict. And procedural justice encompasses the rules of the game for regulating the inevitable conflict between different perspectives, expectations, and tolerances in people's lives. The police officer's job does not include attempting to make people's conflicting expectations come together and agree within some overarching conception of what is good (the good in life). Rather, the job involves, where possible, finding ways to enable people to coexist. Citizens don't have to agree, they don't have to reconcile their differences, and they don't have to find common ground. It is neither possible nor desirable that their mutually hostile concepts of good should be combined to form a single and agreed-upon concept. The justice meted out by the police on the street can only clear the path to recognition of compromises between incompatible desires and ideas of what is better. See box 3-4.

Police officers cannot solve all the problems of the world that are created because of diverse opinions, experiences, and possibilities. But they can and must attempt to deal fairly with the conflict that arises. The police are umpires on the street. They referee the game of life, attempting, if they are competent professionals, to have as little impact as possible on the final score while making sure the game is played fairly. Continuing with the sports metaphor, some people will win and some will lose, when the final score is counted. But it is neither possible nor a good idea to think that the police will influence people's views of the good (what type of formations to run, using a football analogy) or decide who is worthy of being treated fairly and who is not (directly influencing the game's score).

Thus, the basic human experience involves the demand for justice. It is a naturally occurring demand in all of us. And the human experience also creates an individual idea of the good. We need a "free society," and we need "justice" so that each person's individual idea of the good can flourish.

Box 3-4

Two Types of Justice

- **Substantive Justice:** Society's Specific Rules of Conduct

   (Examples include rape and murder laws in the penal code)

- **Procedural Justice:** The "Rules of the Game"

   (Examples include the Miranda decision, which requires that suspects be advised of their rights)

Concepts of substantive justice are derived from particular concepts of the good. Under what conditions is execution justified? Under what circumstances is it justifiable for an abused woman to shoot the abusing husband? Can abortion be justified? These are questions of substantive justice, and universal agreement cannot be expected.

However, universal agreement can be expected, in the name of rationality, on the methods of fair argument, of weighing claims and counter-claims, of arbitrating between the conflicting answers to these questions when an answer is needed for public purposes, and of—in the arena of the police officer—how a citizen ought to be treated, no matter what he or she is accused of having done.

3-2c The Good

As is true with procedural justice, the moral notion of the good grows naturally out of a basic human experience and not out of a belief or theory that all people "know" and universally accept. People have very different ideas, for example, of how important education, financial security, exercise, and entertainment are to living a good life. And they not only value these concepts to different extents, but they also possess different definitions of them altogether.

For example, some people consider "getting an education" to entail learning about life in general (in the "school of hard knocks") and/or becoming educated about their professions or occupations. Others consider that truly educated people are those who go as far as they can in the academic world and learn as much as they can about every subject in which they engage. Similarly, some people are entertained by the opera or the symphony and others by tractor pulls and Roller Derby. Often, people who love one will detest the other. In a free society, we must acknowledge that these types of differences exist, are the right of every person to possess, and are, indeed, part of the fabric that makes life in our society interesting. Put another way, if everyone liked the same things and prioritized them equally, life would be pretty boring. See box 3-5.

Box 3-5

A Problem with Diverse Views About the Good

America is a diverse society with more than 150 different ethnic and religious traditions coming together and seeking to exist in some sort of harmony. Our argument that there is no one, universal concept of the good rests upon a central American theme: the freedom of the individual to hold, voice, and act upon his or her own opinions, views, and philosophy. But there is a problem with this idea that cannot be ignored.

Orthodox religion takes the opposite approach to understanding the good. That is, orthodox religions claim there is one universal good for all people. The Bible, the Koran, and the Torah in particular—the holy books of the three orthodox, "modern" religions—each takes the perspective that to be a good person is to understand the one, true concept of the good and to behave in one particular way. Some believe the Ten Commandments, for example, are aimed at all people at all times with no qualifications or reservations. Everyone must accept them and cleave to them.

There is no room in such a view for the type of diversity that we are discussing. While we certainly do not want to insist that police officers do not, or worse cannot, cleave to their own religious faiths, it must be understood that in policing a diverse, free, tolerant society, police officers cannot foist their own religious views—specifically with reference to the good—upon others. American legal and even religious tradition demands just the opposite—that tolerance for the ideas, philosophies and worldviews of others be a central tenet in how society operates.

With specific reference to police work then, American tradition demands that the police not behave in a way that attempts to underwrite any universal idea of the good. Police officers may hold their own views and behave accordingly in their private lives, but they may not police as if these views are supposed to be accepted by everyone.

In a free society, ferociously held interests and passions are often reconcilable or compromised through rational calculations. But ferociously held concepts of the good and of right and wrong are not. No mechanism of rational choice can help in moral conflicts as they might with the conflicts over competing interests. The idea of justice, then, is embedded in an unavoidable predicament: the necessity of agreement by discussion—without force or outright surrender—between antagonistic people who have clashed because one or both are not getting their way because of their different concepts of the good.

To review, people's different concepts of the good come from the human experience, from the tendency to praise, to blame, to want something better, to be guided by ideals, to focus on the important, to ignore the trivial, and so on. And the thread that links the human experience to the individual concept of the good is this idea of possibility—what might have been and what might be in our lives.

In section 3-2, "Moral Judgment," we have discussed the general notion of moral judgment in terms of "possibilities" and the moral concepts of "justice" and "the good." We have argued that our moment-by-moment experience is alive with possibility, charged with the electricity of what can happen and with the feeling of responsibility that comes from knowing that the possibilities are our possibilities. Being allowed to make realistic judgments about our possibilities and the way we want to live requires being dealt with fairly, that is, justly. This is the only condition under which people can pursue the good of their lives.

3-3 Discretionary Decisions and the Idea of Character

The idea that a police officer's character is critical to the integrity of the justice system turns on one central reality. Police officers possess a tremendous amount of discretionary decision-making power. In terms of the impact their decision can have on the lives of citizens, the police have more discretionary power than any other actors in the entire American legal and political system. The police have the power, right on the street, to completely ignore deviant behavior and not bring a person into the grips of the criminal justice system. No other actor in the process can have this impact on the lives of people, because once a public defender, prosecutor, judge, or probation officer focuses on a citizen's behavior, the citizen has already entered the system. Only the cop on the beat has the power to keep a person completely out of the system.

Police officers regularly make decisions to arrest or not to arrest, to use force or not to use force, to intervene in altercations or to leave people alone to solve their own problems. These decisions are made on the street, often alone, and often at night, without any witnesses. Particularly when the decision is to ignore deviance and leave people alone, police officer actions are not reviewed by others. Thus, this tremendous power is not accountable to anyone else. So, to whom is the police officer accountable?

The answer is that most of the time, under most circumstances, the discretionary decisions of police officers are accountable to the personal ethical standards of the individual police officer. Thus, the focus on police officer character is critical. Police officers, faced with arguments on both sides of an altercation between citizens, will make choices about what to do based on their understanding of what constitutes justice, the rule of law, the practically achievable, and most important, the good in life. There is no escaping this reality.

Police officer character molds and drives the life of the law. The character of individual officers gives a certain meaning to society's norms and values. Police officers who possess good character, who understand the difference between truth and distortion, and who have a firm fix on what it means to do good in life, are the guarantors of justice on the streets of America. Their discretionary decision-making power makes them the critical people in determining what the law truly means (what it looks like, what it feels like) in the lives of American citizens.

3-4 Revisiting the Idea That "The Police Are the Law"

We suggested in chapter 1 that it is time for modern, intelligent, educated police officers to struggle to understand what the good life means, reflecting on what constitutes virtue and formulating specific ideas about what it means to have good character. This is not just an academic exercise that was of interest to the ancient Greeks. Such reflection directly targets what it means to be a good person and live a meaningful life today and always.

For police officers, people who exercise a great deal of power over the lives of others, such discussions and analyses are critical. As we said earlier in chapter 3, no amount of physical agility, intelligence, training, or street sense can make a person a good police officer. Only when he or she has integrated all of this talent, skill, and information into an individual, character-driven, working personality that resides within a solidly based professional ethic can true competence and professionalism develop.

Thus, we expand our idea that the police are the law. The law must have a conscience that keeps its operations consistent with American ideals of justice. The law must be a living entity that is not stagnant but that responds to the heartbeat of life on the street, to people's hopes and dreams. The law must be tempered with a feeling for life's circumstances that allows human empathy to modify its application. The law must be underwritten with an understanding of the practical, sometimes violent and ugly, nature of the drama of real life. And the police officer whose character is formed with all of these ideals at its base is the person most likely to bring these dynamics into play. Judges, attorneys, probation offi-cers, parole officers, and any number of other actors in the legal system can help to bring these ideals to life. But the cop on the beat is the state agent who is closest to the lives of all citizens.

Summary

Chapter 3 brings several ideas together. The first is one of our central themes, the idea that in the lives of many if not most people, the decisions of the police define the law. The second is that because there are multiple, conflicting, and vague roles for the police to play, and because the police are so often faced with conflicting arguments and delicate balances of rights, those decisions are very often made with reference to the ethical perspec-tives of individual police officers. Third, such ethical perspectives are direct expressions of the character of those individuals who become police officers.

Thus, the integrity of the law is dependent upon the integrity of the individual police officer. The consistency of the law is the consistency of the police officer. The fairness, objectivity, and justice of the operations of the legal system are all dependent upon the good character of police officers.

Topics for Discussion

1. In Aristotle's terms, who are your "exemplars?" Who are your role mod-els? Discuss where and how we get our "heroes" today.
2. A rather critical differentiation is made between "equality of treatment" and "justice." Create your own examples of how justice might not be served by equal treatment. How might injustice be created by treating people in exactly equal ways?
3. Police officers often think that they are constantly under scrutiny and being watched. But this is a myth. Discuss why police officers are taught to believe this myth—why it might be a good thing that many believe it and why it might be a bad thing. How does this discussion plug into our analysis of the importance of individual police officer character?

The Development of Character

4

forced or delayed development molds your personality traits.

> *"We're looking for a few good men."*
> — Recruitment Slogan for the United States Marine Corps

Outline

4-1 Being Yourself … On Purpose
4-2 Emotions As a Form of Understanding
4-3 Ethical Perception
Summary
Topics for Discussion

Freud 3 Stages:
-Oral: Pleasure, Derived through, Nursing/pacifier (0-18 m)
9 month is when u starting weaning. fixation 12 months
start cereal, forced or delayed development (fixation)

-Nal-18m-3 years: Focused -Eliminating waste, control, personality trait
power over others. You are rewarded for your behavior
hallic - 3to6 years: general fixation (the fact that boys+girls
are different). Sexual divience
atency-by-puberty: Sexual identity is repressed or
upressed. Act out by engaging in same sex or abusive
lationships.
-nital-Puberty

61

In the discussion about the critical importance of police officer character (chapter 3), we made general reference to character as a concept. It was important to illustrate how important it is for the police officer to have a perspective on life that is underwritten by an understanding of ethics, the central element in character. But in a more practical, day-to-day sense, how do we get character?

Chapter 4 will delve more deeply into what character is, how we obtain it, and how it operates. This discussion will often seem unrelated to police work per se because we must amplify our considerations of police officer character and ethics with a more worldly understanding of these concepts as they relate to everyone—police officers and citizens alike. Then, and only then, can we move to focus directly on the police.

Throughout this work, we have stressed that character is the most critical aspect of ethical conduct and, therefore, of police professionalism. "Character" is the term given to a person's enduring traits that affect how a person sees the world, understands it, and acts in it. These traits explain not merely why someone acts a certain way now but why someone can always be counted on to act in a certain way. In this sense, character gives a special sort of accountability and pattern to human action.

Character covers a wide range of traits other than moral ones. Beside moral virtues such as honesty, courage, and loyalty, people's characters include traits that, in one way or another, contribute to their general well being, their aptitude for success in life, their readiness to learn, their inclination to pay attention and the sort of things that tend to get their attention, as well as their likelihood for happiness. But the part of character that pertains to ethics is the most deeply rooted in our humanity because it involves that which animals lack—a pronounced understanding of right and wrong.

Our discussion will focus on the elements of character and some of the positive, conscious things people can do to promote good character within themselves.

"You gotta be yourself, kid. But on purpose."
— Paul Newman to Tom Cruise in *The Color of Money*

4-1 Being Yourself ... On Purpose

People do not live their lives automatically or by instinct. A wolf does not try to be a good wolf. A wolf does not take stock in its life, resolve to be a better wolf, and act accordingly. It just does what it must to stay alive.

But people's lives are never-ending projects for them. Unlike animals, people must try to be themselves. A great irony of the human condition is that we try to live a certain way, try to be seen and thought of by others in

Box 4-1

Deliberateness and Legal Responsibility

As a matter of legal fact, this idea of deliberateness is so thoroughly webbed into our common understanding of human responsibility that the legal definition of an "act" is "deliberate, knowing behavior." Generally speaking, a person is held responsible by the law only for an offense he or she knowingly commits in terms of the realistic possibilities available to him or her.

Mental impairment mitigates responsibility and changes the nature of the act. An underage child falls into a different category of offender because age qualifies against responsibility. The law takes the view that responsibility does not attach to coerced behavior; taking the cash out of the till with the thief's gun pointed at your head is not something for which you will be held responsible.

Taken together, these ideas mean that the law requires and expects people to live in the deliberate way that we are suggesting.

a certain light. The athlete strives to "stay focused." The worried single mother tells herself, "I've got to stay upbeat in front of the kids." The actor repeats the mantra, "Stay in character." The good teacher tries to resist becoming cynical and to continue to do the best for pupils. Police officers being pressured by corrupt partners must tell themselves, "Remember who you are." We all want to be thought of in a certain way. We remember what others have said about us and we act. This is all very deliberate. We are being ourselves, but on purpose. See box 4-1.

People see their lives in terms of an array of real or imagined possibilities over which they exercise some control. We live in the tension between *what is* and *what might be.* This tension explains our hopes and fears, plans and dreams. It explains everything we do; it explains the coherent and unified, identifiable, individual quality of our lives. When we focus on the so-called moral virtues (honesty, generosity, courage, etc.), it is important to remember that the basis of these virtues includes those features of our makeup that enable us to live a purposeful life.

There is a certain dramatic quality to all of our lives in the sense that we are often conscious of playing a role, of trying to *be* somebody. Police officers want to look like police officers. They want, for example, to look firm, resolute, and tough. Trying to look that way means they are trying to be that way. Being a certain kind of cop is not automatic; it is not something that is simply conferred upon us when we are given a badge. It is something we deliberately, consciously do, and to one degree or another, it is something we continue to work at. We are conscious of who we are and who we want to be. But there is a gap between the two, and we try to close that gap. Furthermore, police officers live with the awareness that it is not guaranteed they will succeed. They have to work at it and work hard.

Our care about what we do takes the form of filling the gap between what we think we are and what we want to be—or how we think we are seen and how we want to be seen. In revealing what is important to us, our care shows who we are trying to be. Our personhood is not fixed in advance, and so greatly does that fact matter to us that it organizes our every move. This is a mark of our character.

While a great deal of who we are is determined early in life, we nevertheless change and adapt and grow over the course of our lives. It is only the true defeatists, the people who have lost themselves to the idea that they cannot change due to some kind of external forces, who believe they have no control over who they are and their own characters.

4-2 Emotions As a Form of Understanding

This entire discussion about care and interest points to the fact that emotions as well as reason ground the moral virtues. Our discussion about the relation between possibilities, personal identity, and care shows that emotions are themselves modes of moral response. Our emotions determine what is morally relevant to us and, in some cases, what is required of us. When police officers see a gang member "tagging" a city bus, a drunk driver careening through traffic, or a tourist who has just had his or her wallet stolen, don't those officers have an immediate and visceral response to what they see? This emotional response is a gauge of what interests them, of what they find significant in the scene, and of what they understand about it. To act rightly is to be emotionally engaged—it is to act in a way that brings to bear the lessons of the heart and not just those of a calm intellect. An act motivated by the right reason but lacking in the right feeling is merely correct. It does not necessarily show good character. See box 4-2.

When we recognize that we have done something wrong that is of moral consequence to another, we not only feel bad for them, we feel remorse. Our remorse is our recognition of the wrong we have done and

Box 4-2

A Paradox About Police Officers

It is commonly thought that police officers are cynical types, expecting the worst in people. They see all of the worst behavior humanity has to offer and begin to expect the worst from everyone. The drunkard, the gang member, the insane person, the true degenerate, the vicious predator, the ignorant victim, the self-centered thief, and a host of other negative people necessarily come into the lives of police officers.

But oddly enough, a number of studies indicate that most people become police officers because they want to help people. No matter how jaded they may end up eventually, most police officers begin their work with this in mind.

It is a paradox that caring for victims, helping the truly vulnerable, and wanting the world to be different—working toward just that end—combines with these negative experiences to make many officers removed and aloof. In other words, it is not that police officers do not care about people—but precisely that they do care about people—that, in the long run, makes many of them lose faith in people.

---

of the person we have become in so doing. This reveals that when a man hits his wife, for example, he gets more than he bargained for; he gets himself as a wife-beater. When a wife lies to her husband, she gets herself as a liar. Whether we like it or not, that's part of the deal we make when we do something: we become what we do. The rest of the world recognizes this about us and, even though we may try to deny or rationalize it, we recognize it, too. What else accounts for the rationalization and the common effort to shift blame?

To feel remorse is to judge that we did something wrong. Remorse is not so much caused by understanding, as if there were first the insight into what we did and then the feeling of remorse for it. Rather, remorse is a form of understanding the seriousness of what we did and what we have morally become.

It is a common experience for us to note that in situations where remorse seems called for, people's lack of remorse shows a lack in their depth of understanding. Or, in showing that the situation had a different significance for them than it did for us, their lack of remorse shows that what stood out to us about the situation was not real to them.

The point here is to note that what we understand to be the reality of a situation is a direct function of its significance for us, of what interests us about it. Our emotional response is our grasp of what matters. We react emotionally the way we do because we are seized with a certain reality—outrage at seeing the strong prey upon the weak, the good person unjustly treated, the victim bleeding in the street, the child unprotected from harm by ignorant parents, and so on. Just as remorse is a form of understanding the seriousness of what we have done, so too, pity is a form of understanding the pain of another. Emotions such as remorse and pity are natural aspects of moral judgment.

A further implication of what we say about the whole complex of care in our lives is that moral response does not assume impartiality. In most of the professions that deal with people (medicine, social work, nursing, teaching, police work), we hear a lot of talk about being "objective." While it is true medical decisions or the application of the law must be done fairly and in an impartial manner, we are arguing here that impartially, in the sense of not giving preferential treatment, does not imply that the professional must not care about people.

One of the criticisms leveled at all of these "caring" professions is that the people with whom professionals interact tend to be seen as cases rather than as people. This tendency develops because, as if on an assembly line, patients and students and citizens move by the professionals and, in the name of impartiality, their individuality is not acknowledged. Impartiality is necessary in the sense that professionals cannot show favoritism. But here we are saying that impartiality can go too far; it can develop a certain indifference or even a cynicism in the professional that impedes the ability to make moral decisions.

Seeing the morally relevant features of a situation in and of itself shows moral sensibility and moral character and is a part of a morally appropriate response. Pursuing the right response does not begin with making choices but with recognizing circumstances relevant to some desired end that counts as good. Knowing how to see the relevant particulars is a mark of morality. Character is expressed in what one sees as much as in what one does. Therefore, morality begins in character.

When a police officer notices an incident that calls for attention, the ability to see the relevant particulars of the scene is as much a matter of emotional awareness as it is a rational matter. Often, officers see what they see because of and through their emotions. So, for example, a feeling of indignation makes the cop sensitive to the cruelty of a mugger, just as pity opens the eyes to the pain of the person mugged. The officer's emotional dispositions create a relevant point of view for seeing what is important

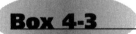

An Example of Police Jadedness

In a recent example in New York City, police officers stood by at a Puerto Rican celebration and let a gang of men molest and rape women. What did these officers see when they looked at the incident? Did they consider the molesters' actions "funny"? Did they rationalize "that's the way those people behave"? Did they avoid getting involved and doing their jobs because "women like that kind of thing"? What does the fact that dozens of officers took no action reveal about what they understood, about their response, and about their character?

in the situation. The professional officer notices feelings that might otherwise go unnoticed by a detached or uncaring person—witness the cops at the Puerto Rican festivities discussed in box 4-3. Emotions, then, are absolutely vital to an intelligent, ethical perspective in life. Moreover, emotions are educable. Just as a child learns the multiplication tables, dates, and historic names, we can learn what our feelings mean. When it matters to us, such as when we are trying to be good police officers, we can learn to feel differently about people's life situations and perspectives.

4-3 Ethical Perception

There is an important difference between appropriate and inappropriate anger, appropriate and inappropriate fear, and so on. When anger is inappropriate, it is excessive or not called for. That is, there is a gap between what a person understands, which the anger expresses, and what he or she ought to understand. Police officers are regularly angry (outraged) by unlawful behavior—such as being confronted by a burglar who steals into a family's home and takes precious possessions—but this anger must be appropriately channeled into the desire to take legal action. It cannot rationalize "curbside justice" by allowing the cop to deliver a beating as punishment for such behavior. This first kind of anger (driven by empathy for the victim) is not only understandable, but it is an important part of what motivates the professional officer to act. The second kind of anger (driven by a desire for revenge) is dangerous for the professional as it rationalizes the use of excessive force and convolutes the entire meaning of the justice system.

Before officers decide how to act, they must first understand that the situation requires action—something the cops in the New York incident described in box 4-3 did not see. The decision to act will come from a realistic reading of the situation. And those things that stand out as being important are determined by an officer's moral sensibility. Therefore, much of the work of good character rests in knowing how to construct a situation, how to describe and classify what is going on. This takes practice. And in doing this practice from day to day, police officers have no good reason to be bullheaded about the way they see things.

Only a fool believes his or her way is the one and only way to judge situations. The truth is very much the opposite; the desire to be a decent person—the desire to be a competent police officer—requires that we remain critical of ourselves. We must be open to inquiry and questioning, from ourselves and from others; that requires us to continue to reflect on the purpose of our conduct. Only in reflecting on conduct in actual situations on the beat can police officers reflect on themselves, on their lives, and on their professional competence. "Did I do the right thing? Could I have solved this situation differently, in a more just manner? Did I really have to use force, or could I have talked the kid into the car?" These types of questions need to be asked again and again as the officer changes, grows in competence, and learns.

Thus, we can have control over our emotions. We know how this works. Through collaboration with other officers and citizens, through listening to and identifying with the viewpoints of others, an officer's vision becomes expanded and enlarged. This moral vision, and with it the ability to detect relevant facts, improves. The open-minded officer comes to learn different ways to read situations and different questions to ask to see the scene with improved clarity and understanding. *How to see* becomes as much a matter of inquiry as *what to do*. Such inquiry and dialogue establish the route to long-term understanding. As is true in all occupations, in law enforcement there is a pronounced tendency to think there is one way to handle a detail—and that in an officer's early days on the street, he or she learns this one way. We are saying this idea is foolish and that in operating this way, officers limit their ability to continue to grow and to become the best, most competent professionals they can be.

The key is to cultivate a pride in remaining open to questions. Probably no one thing is more telling of a person's character than the ability to be critical of himself or herself. All the other moral virtues and the possibility of learning or improving rest upon remaining open to the world. Every person has much to learn from life. Wisdom consists in accepting that fact.

"There are no great men. There are only ordinary men, like you and me, who sometimes must surmount great challenges."
— President Harry Truman

Summary

Our character produces plans that express an overall unity of purpose, an identifiable plot line, in the story of our lives. Moral judgment is best understood as a set of judgments about possibilities because the decisions we make involve assessing our possibilities in terms of the way they fit into our overall concept of what is good. Many of the choices we make concern long-term intentions, and such future thinking reveals the kinds of people we are trying to be. This is what is meant by the claim that choices exhibit character.

People live their lives in the tension and openness created by the flow of such possibilities, and for that reason the concepts of justice and the good are bedrock principles in a moral life. These moral concepts flow directly from the relationships, experiences, and predicaments of our lives. They constitute images of the different possibilities available to people and their differing notions of the good. These moral concepts do not come from some abstract, universal ideas. Because police work is carried out at the level of procedural justice, police competence is unavoidably bound to good character.

Emotions are a critical element in moral understanding because we perceive the morally relevant facts of a situation through our emotional responses. And our emotional responses also reveal what we morally understand about both a given situation and ourselves. To a great extent, we choose our character, because our emotions are educable. That is, we can change the way we feel, the way we respond, as we become aware of what it means to us and about us.

Having done a significant amount of reflecting about character, what it is and its importance, we now turn to two chapters that will introduce several ethical theories that discuss how to make moral judgments. As opposed to our character-based discussion here, we will now discuss rule-based sets of principles for approaching ethical questions. The difference in these two approaches will become clear as we proceed through the next two discussions.

Topics for Discussion

1. One of chapter 4's subjects is the idea that we strive to be somebody and to be perceived in a certain way. Discuss how it is that we want to be seen by others on the street in our roles as police officers. What is it we are trying to be like out there?

2. Discuss the difference between being objective and impartial (not being "too emotional" as professionals) and being so remote from human suffering that one doesn't "care." How can dealing with people in crisis develop a jadedness and cynicism that make an officer ineffective at seeing what is important in a given situation?

3. Discuss how to handle a detail involving a large group of partying teenagers. First, discuss locker-room truisms, "rules of thumb," that you have heard about how to do such a job. Second, critique these rules of thumb and consider alternative ways to do the job. Note that the reason for having this discussion is to emphasize the idea there is more than one way to handle any type of detail—there are, in common vernacular, "many ways to skin a cat."

Chapter 5

Ethical Formalism

*"You don't do things right some of the time.
You do them right all of the time."*
— Vince Lombardi, Football Coach

Outline

Ethical theories can be divided into several major categories along different lines of distinction. For our discussion, we will emphasize one basic differentiation. Some ethical theories formulate and encourage the individual to follow absolute rules about what is the good and about a person's duty to behave in a certain manner. In ancient history, this idea had its beginning in religion—"It is right because God said so." Consider, for example, the biblical story of Abraham's readiness to kill his son, Isaac (Genesis 22). See box 5-1.

Today, these absolutist theories are most prominently represented by "ethical formalism." Immanuel Kant was the founder of this school of thought, and his theory is based on the idea that people investigate principles of conduct, norms of behavior, and specific rules (some of which are laws) for human interactions. Modern sociologists suggest that people don't find these principles—whether bestowed by God, as religion teaches, or intuited by us as the very condition for rational conduct, as Kaut argued—but that together, collectively, we invent them. These principles/rules involve absolute duties to behave in certain ways under all circumstances.

In calculating what to do when making choices between behavioral options, the second type of theory involves taking into consideration the specific situation a choice presents. Such situational theories of ethics are not absolutist. On the contrary, they suggest it is most logical (and morally defensible) to make choices that may vary from situation to situation—driven by a concern for the consequences of such choices. Such a theory is that of utilitarianism, treated in chapter 6.

5-1 Ethical Formalism: Kant's Theory of Duty

People who take conscience to be their guide are essentially Kantians. Whether they realize it or not, these people believe that the right, the obligatory, the morally good, is determined by only one thing: the intention that lies behind an action, the reason for which it was done. They believe the whole moral worth of an act comes from the nature of its motivation and not from what the act brings about (or its consequences). They believe that what the person tries to do has moral value, not what the person causes by the act. In focusing exclusively upon intention, ethical formalists believe there is an absolute principle (the Categorical Imperative) upon which ethical choices must be based. No consequence-based calculations enter in to this absolutist view of duty.

Kant pointed out there are many factors involved in successfully accomplishing something. Over most of these factors, a person exercises no direct control. Through no fault of their own, people may not be skillful enough or may not know enough to succeed in accomplishing a good

Box 5-1

Religious Ethics

Religion presents a somewhat different set of views about ethics. The world's great, organized religions suggest that, rather than being made by humans, ethics are God given. That is, rather than being discovered by intelligent human beings, definitions of the good and rules of right conduct are given to the human race by some supreme authority. This authority might be a God, the gods, Mother Nature, the Great Spirit, or divinely inspired prophets. Human beings find out about these rules from the great religious works of history such as the Bible, the Koran, or the Torah; from great prophets such as Moses, Jesus, Mohammed, or Buddha; or from living sources such as priests and other religious authorities. The rules that religion brings to us are absolute pronouncements from the ultimate authority and are not alterable in any way.

We do not reject this idea. But in discussing how to fashion an ethic to live by, we are going to focus on principles and issues of character that are determined by people themselves. Part of our ethic involves avoiding absolute pronouncements in favor of a more practical, situation-guided idea of how a person develops his or her own character and makes choices with regard to how to behave.

---

deed. Other people may not cooperate or may work against the person. Or circumstances may get in the way. As important as these factors obviously are, they cannot count in assessing the moral worth of an act because morality relates to a person's frame of mind, to his or her "heart," and not to facts about the world. Morally speaking, doing something for the right reason is all that matters.

We agree with Kant in this: there are other considerations that make an action right, good, or obligatory besides the goodness or badness of its consequences (the outcome). We agree that certain features of an act itself make the act right—for example, the fact that it keeps a promise or it is just. We might also agree that sometimes other facts about an act make it right or obligatory—for example, that it is commanded by God, by our religious beliefs, or by our patriotism.

With specific regard to Kant's view of morality, he has provided a rule called the Categorical Imperative that tests the moral validity of any action. (See box 5-2.) The rule is "categorical" because it applies universally to all situations. It is "imperative" because it has the force of a law of reason and is not in any respect optional. It is absolute. Kant gave three

Box 5-2

One Formulation of Kant's Categorical Imperative

"Act only on that maxim which you can at the same time will to be a universal law."

Kant said that when deciding what is the right thing to do in any given situation, we must act as if we were making a universal rule that would be followed by all people facing similar facts and making similar decisions.

formulations of the Categorical Imperative, but we shall restrict ourselves to only one of the three: "Act only on that maxim which you can at the same time will to be a universal law." In this statement, Kant gives the one principle that should control the ethical decisions we make and live by.

With this imperative, Kant was saying several things at once. First, when people do something voluntarily, they must always act on a rule they can formulate or explain to themselves. This means when people act on their own initiative, they must know the reason why. Blind obedience to a rule, not accompanied by an understanding of the intention of the rule, is not satisfactory.

Second, a person is choosing and judging from a morally defensible point of view if, and only if, he or she is willing to universalize his or her maxim (the motive that lies behind the act). That is, people choose to do the right thing only when it is possible to imagine that all others would make the same choice—a rule that should be acted on by everyone in a similar situation, even if they turn out to be on the receiving end. This is the philosopher's version of the Biblical The Golden Rule: "Do unto others as you would have them do unto you."

Third, Kant tells us that doing our duty is to act on maxims we can universalize, and that this has a moral value by definition. That is, irrespective of what consequence it brings to the world, a dutiful act is ethical in and of itself. Having the will to cleave to a duty is to have a good will and this is sufficient to make a person's behavior ethical.

Let us take one of Kant's own examples of how he applies his rule. He supposes a person makes a promise but is ready to break it when it suits his or her purposes. The person's maxim about making promises might be expressed this way: "When it suits me, I will make promises—but also, when it suits me, I will break promises." Kant says a person cannot consistently will that this maxim be universally acted upon. A person can easily "will the lie, but not a universal law to lie." He is saying that people cannot will that they themselves be lied to when it suits someone else's interests. This makes no sense.

Kant is not arguing that a person must keep his or her promises because the results of everyone breaking promises, when convenient to himself or herself, would be bad. (As we will see in chapter 6, this is how a utilitarian would run the argument.) Instead, Kant is contending that you cannot even will such a maxim or rule to be universally acted on because in so doing you would be involved in a contradiction. He is saying that, at the same time, a person cannot: (1) will that people be able to make promises and have them accepted as binding, and (2) will everyone also be free to break promises to suit themselves. Such a maxim is self-defeating. If a person acts on the maxim that to make deceitful promises is acceptable, then the "institution of promise making" becomes meaningless.

Kant's philosophy of ethics thus focuses on the intention behind people's acts. It considers their consequences uncontrollable and, thus, irrelevant. He means to infuse into people the ideal that their duty is absolute. No amount of rationalization, whether it be self-serving or aimed at some community good, can be used to challenge the maxims included in this absolutist perspective of ethics. Right is right, and it is right all the time. See box 5-3.

5-2 The Strengths of Kant's Absolutism

Suppose a police officer, following his or her absolute Kantian duty, arrests a marijuana smoker at a large rock concert. The arrest results in a brawl between police officers and dozens of teenagers. The principles of ethical formalism suggest that, because pot smoking is illegal—everywhere at all times—the arrest was appropriate. Utilitarian logic (which we will discuss in chapter 6) suggests that the consequences of the arrest, a riotous situation that developed out of relative calm, were bad and thus the action taken (the arrest) was wrong. From the utilitarian perspective, even though marijuana smoking is against the law, making an arrest under these circumstances would have negative consequences that outweigh the positive duty to enforce the law absolutely.

The above example is a good one for several reasons. It illustrates a commonplace form of police discretionary decision making. It makes a good case for police officers to use their heads and hearts instead of being

Box 5-3

Absolute Duties

We live in an era where a great deal of emphasis is placed on cultural diversity. One of the problems for Kantians today is that, because different cultures create different norms, values, and laws, there is serious debate about whether or not duties exist that are absolute. Here are some ideas about what might be included in a list of such absolute duties:

- Every child deserves to be loved.
- Married people should cleave to their spouses and forsake all others.
- Parents should protect their children from harm and provide them with food, clothing, shelter, and safety.
- Children should provide the same protections for their parents when they enter old age.
- People must never mistreat animals.
- People must never use others simply to obtain their own ends.
- It is evil to knowingly kill the innocent.

Do you agree with some, most, or many of these "absolute" duties? Can you think of others? Or do you agree that absolute duties might not exist?

---

absolutist in their decision making. It seems, therefore, to make an argument against the principles of ethical formalism. But ethical formalism has strong supporters everywhere in the world. There is good reason to argue that "rules are rules" and, using an old police adage, "we don't make the rules, we just enforce them."

Whether people know it or not, they often argue in support of ethical formalism's absolute principles because they value the rule of law and understand that in discretion lies a problem of huge significance. Too much discretion can mean an end to the rule of law. Allowing rule enforcers, the police in the case of our discussions, to "use their heads" can too often mean they cease to apply the law as it is written. They may use the freedom that discretion creates for them to control the streets in an arbitrary manner. Even when supported by the people in a community or in a neighborhood, the exercise of power without reference to preexisting rules can bring about the sort of tyranny the rule of law was invented to overcome.

Think about the American Revolution. Why did the colonists revolt? One reason was that King George's men had so much power over individual colonists that these soldier-policemen were a law unto themselves. What were then called "writs of assistance" allowed the Redcoats to search any person, house, or business whenever they wanted to, with no reason whatsoever. This practice furnished the reasoning behind the construction of our Constitution's Fourth Amendment and its pronouncements against "unreasonable searches and seizures." The founders of our constitutional form of government loathed this power and feared that it might develop in their new country.

Tyranny is the "exercise of power cruelly or unjustly." The tyrannical rule by a person or group of people who are not accountable to anyone was a part of history for thousands of years before the invention of the idea of law. It was the tyranny of the southern slave system that was the major cause of the Civil War. It was the tyranny of the Japanese and the Nazis that brought America into World War II. And tyranny is still a part of the contemporary world. It was the tyranny of the Serbs that recently brought American troops to Kosovo.

The central idea of democracy is that the people get together, or their elected representatives do, and formulate the rules by which society will be governed. Then, agents of this consensually created state (the police) apply those rules on the street. If the rule appliers exercise so much discretion that they are not actually following the rules, then whoever ends up being arrested will believe he or she has been singled out for unfair treatment. If, in other words, discretion is abused, then the rule of law ends and the rule of cop begins. See box 5-4.

If this abuse of discretion develops, then society ceases to be built upon consensus. And the police become a law unto themselves, as the Redcoats once were. This then refers back to one of our central themes. The police are the law in the realistic sense that their decisions determine what the law means to millions of people. But they must be governed by a commitment, an absolute (Kantian) duty, to serve the law just as they serve society and the people. If they begin to act as if they really are the law in every sense, then the police destroy the essence of what America is: a country ruled by individual freedom, representative democracy, and justice for all.

Thus there are good, practical, legal, and ethical reasons for accepting what Kant says, or at least some of it. But the Kantian, absolutist position

Box 5-4

Khadi Justice

In North Africa, there are tribes that have lived for thousands of years without what we would call a formal legal system. When disputes between individuals arise, instead of trials with juries and judges, problems are brought to the Khadi. The Khadi is the lawgiver. He decides disputes using the general direction of the Koran (the sacred Islamic bible) and his own moral principles. The Khadi answers to no one. His decisions don't have to be consistent, and sometimes they are not. One dispute may be decided one way on one day, and the next day a similar dispute may be decided another way.

People who study comparative legal systems call this type of absolute decision-making power "Khadi Justice." It refers to the ultimate in discretion. No rules, no principles, no laws are referenced—only the personal understanding of the decision maker about what is right serves as the grounds for dispute resolution.

---

has problems associated with it. And it is toward a consideration of those problems that we now turn.

5-3 A Critique of Kant and Absolutism

For all the "rule of law"-related strengths it possesses, Kant's position creates difficulties. We have to be careful, because when we carry out the implications of his position it becomes possible for an action, or rule of conduct, to be morally right even if it does not promote good over evil. That is, the logical extension of focusing on a person's intention is that the morality of an act is not measured by the difference, for good or ill, it makes in the life of anyone. It is right simply because of some other fact about it (e.g., it is commanded by God, or by religious faith, or by the law) or because of its own nature (e.g., it is reasonable). For ethical formalists then, acting in conformity with absolute rules is morally valid whether or not to do so promotes a good or makes a difference in someone's life.

Let us take a police work-related example. A teenager with no criminal record is stopped for being out after curfew. The teen is cooperative, sober, and genuinely apologetic for this behavior. In fact, the officer involved finds that the child was driving home from seeing her ill grandmother after a Tuesday night high school basketball game in which the teen played. Irrespective of any analysis about the interests of justice, the law against curfew demands that the child be cited. An absolutist approach to the duty always to obey the law no matter what the circumstances would suggest to the officer that a citation must be issued. The teen's act was against the law and, therefore, was wrong. The officer's act of issuing a citation invokes the law and is, therefore, right.

Taking this Kantian view, we run into a problem. Any act, by itself, is right or wrong. The act's moral quality is completely determined only by its own moral quality. This is circular logic and suggests that the position is no real position at all.

Put more clearly, we are suggesting that the moral worth of an act must depend, at least in part, on something beyond itself, on something about the real difference it makes in the lives of people. We mean that the morality of an act must be directly linked to the good or evil consequences it produces for someone. It follows that in order to know whether some behavior is right or wrong, one must first know what is good and whether the act in question promotes or is intended to promote what is good. Otherwise, how would one know what behavior was right?

In the example cited above, the officer's choice to issue a citation must be related to the impact that it might have on a teenager with an otherwise clear record. Sticking to the absolute duties of enforcing the law at all times might very well impact the teen's life in a way that is not morally defensible.

A separate problem with Kant arises from conflicts between duties. For example, one duty, according to Kant, is to tell the truth. Another is to protect people from harm. Unfortunately, it is possible for these two duties to conflict with each other. It is possible, in other words, that lying might help someone in trouble. Would Kant lie to a Gestapo agent who was looking to arrest Jews if he (Kant) knew where they were hiding? One may very well be able to will a specific rule that permits lies in a certain kind of situation (like this one)—"It is okay to lie to Gestapo agents, who are up to no good." But you cannot will a universal law that blankets all exceptions to the law of truth telling. Such a maxim might read, "Tell the truth, unless you think it's best not to." Such a maxim is no maxim at all.

Furthermore, even if we admit that the criterion of the Categorical Imperative rules out certain actions as immoral (for example, lying or deceitful promise making), must we agree that all our moral duties can be established this way? Is the "universality" test enough? We think it is not, especially for the police officer.

Consider loners who don't like people and wish to exercise the freedom to be left completely alone in life. We can readily imagine such people being able to will the universal maxim "People should not help others in need"—even when it is they who are in need. To follow such a maxim would be a disastrous idea for police officers. For the police to operate under the maxim that they ought not to help people would be for the central role of the police to be abrogated.

Another problem is that Kant does not tell us how to determine whether rules are moral rules or not. The "rule" that "you should always button the bottom button first" certainly has nothing to do with morals. But it is a rule of thumb that many observe. In our discussions about character (chapters 3 and 4), we pointed out that morality begins with the recognition of a moral situation, of morally relevant facts, and recognition that a certain kind of response is required. Kant's test of maxims does not help us at all with this problem of determining what are moral issues.

Thus, it seems for maxims to be considered moral duties, it is not enough that you be able to will your maxims to be universal. Since Kant's ethical theory is not concerned with the promotion of good in the world (good consequences, that is) but only with intentions, his idea of universalization reduces to nothing more than a requirement to act in a fashion that is logically consistent with what one wills or wishes. The mere fact that your behavior is consistent with your ideals is certainly not enough to make behavior ethical.

For Kant, rationality—not the goodness brought into people's lives—is the most important feature of morality. This is to praise rationality for its own sake. A strictly Kantian police officer, then, when coming upon a man who has murdered his wife, can only say to him, "You're a traitor to reason! You've violated the rational nature of your wife!" Thus, there is more to the moral point of view than being willing to universalize one's rules. Kant and his followers—focusing on rationality and consistency only—fail to see this fact.

One additional problem for a democratic system is presented by Kant's absolute formulations. Following rules in an absolute way and cleaving to the absolute duty to obey the law can create terrible consequences for people when the law is unjust. When this happens, and history is full of examples, Kantians can be guilty of ignoring higher notions of justice and the good in favor of blind obedience to rules.

Box 5-5

The Nuremberg Trials

After World War II, some of the powerful Nazis who were responsible for sending millions to death camps and to the gas chambers were put on trial. The defense some of them presented was that they were only following the laws of their country at the time (the 1930s and early 1940s). It was, in fact, true that behavior such as fraternization between Jews and Gentiles had been made a crime in Germany at that time. Such crimes were punishable by being sent to the camps. Sex between these races was a crime. These are only two examples of what the law said in Nazi Germany.

Political scientists who study the period tell us that, in the early years of the Nazi reign, these laws were very popular with a majority of Germans. In fact, Adolph Hitler had been very popular and obtained power through the democratic process in Germany in 1932. The question for us here is, what happens when, through the democratic process, laws are passed that are immoral? What happens when a majority of people holds such racist ideas and turns them into laws? This creates what political scientists call "the tyranny of the majority."

Does a law enforcer have a higher duty than to enforce the will of the people as represented in written laws? Did good Germans have a moral obligation to ignore the laws of their land and behave in ways that they considered moral and just, irrespective of what the absolute dictates of German law (in the Nazi era) said?

One of the paradoxes of law is that the enforcement of democratically instituted laws can sometimes be just as tyrannical as the enforcement of the wishes of a few all-powerful people (czars, kings, and dictators). That is, the majority does not always make laws that are just and equitable.

In the American south, for one hundred years after the Civil War, a system of segregation kept blacks in poverty and sent their children to poor schools while most whites lived in relative ease. In Europe, for hundreds of years, the Jews were forced to live in ghettos and were denied the rights of ordinary citizenship. For generations, Irish Catholics were not allowed to vote, own land, or send their children to school. In each of these examples, a majority of the population agreed with these policies and made laws supporting this racism. Thus, democracy is no guaranteed cure for injustice and inhumanity. See box 5-5.

Box 5-6

Kant—Pros and Cons

The Strengths of Absolute Rule Application

- It ensures equal treatment of people similarly situated.
- It develops a respect for the law and for law appliers (police).
- It limits the impact of personal prejudice.
- It makes the law understandable, consistent, and (thus) fair.

The Drawbacks of Absolute Rule Application

- It allows majorities to persecute minorities.
- It does not promote good in people's lives.
- It can inhibit "justice" by not properly discriminating between people.
- It says nothing about how to "see" a situation, to recognize the moral significance of a situation.

Thus, absolute, Kantian obedience to the law can be disastrous for minority rights and for the interests of justice. As we shall see in chapter 6, there are ethical schools of thought that approach moral decision making with a situational view. Such systems as utilitarianism encourage the individual to focus on doing good in a way that takes into account the substantial impact (the consequences) of one's choices on the lives of others and on the good of the community

In summation, Kant's philosophy has several major drawbacks. First, it does not help us with conflicting duties. Second, it cannot allow for reasonable exceptions. Third, we cannot tell whether a maxim is a moral one or not. And fourth, minority rights (that reference higher moral principles) can be sacrificed in the name of obedience to duty. See box 5-6.

Summary

The thrust of chapter 5's discussion goes in two opposite directions. On the one hand, we have sided with ethical formalists and agreed that the objectivity and fairness of the rule of law is necessary to make sure individual prejudice does not rule the streets. To best organize a system that in a just way determines what sorts of conduct are acceptable, a society must be ruled by laws that are administered on the streets in a fair manner by people who are accountable for how they apply those absolute rules. They are accountable, in a democracy, to the people who wrote/made the laws.

On the other hand, rules of conduct are almost invariably too rigid. They do not make allowances for all of the variables of life, for people's strengths and weaknesses, for those who attempt to do the right thing but fall short due to poverty, ignorance, and fate. Absolute rules do not do a very good job, in short, of determining whether the conduct of human beings is acceptable or not. They are not alive enough, sympathetic enough, flexible enough, or realistic enough to be applicable to real-life situations all of the time.

The mother who speeds while taking her child to the hospital emergency room, the first-time shoplifter, the man who hits his wife's lover, the homeless person who steals a coat to stay alive on a winter night—all of these are examples of people who would be arrested under an absolutist system. And they are, equally, examples of people who might be left alone by a flexible, thoughtful, and arguably more just system that was designed to have some insight into the human heart. There are "exceptions to the rule," something for which Kant makes no allowances.

So (1) the police must cleave to the rule of law, and (2) the absolute application of rules (laws) has severe drawbacks associated with it. What are we to make of this dichotomy? The answer is that the law, the absolute rules written down in the penal code, needs to be viewed by the professional police officer as one tool in an arsenal of tools used to maintain order, to protect lives and property, and to serve the community. When tempered by honest, intelligent, educated, ethical professionals through the screen of their discretionary decisions, the law is useful in creating a safe, livable atmosphere on the street wherein people may pursue their own visions of the good life.

In using the law as a tool in the effort to create such an atmosphere, the police promote justice, equality, and freedom. They understand the reasoning behind thinking that the law must be absolute and, equally, they understand the reasoning behind the idea that the law must be aimed at creating happiness for the greatest number of people on a day-to-day basis (see chapter 6). This most democratic of ethical principles is our next stop along the road to developing a fully enriched understanding of police ethics.

Topics for Discussion

1. Discuss the suggested list of "absolute duties" in box 5-3. Do you agree with this list? Would you add other duties to it? Would you exclude some of those suggestions presented?
2. Discuss police-work-related examples of how different duties can conflict. How can the duty to apply the law in an absolute manner conflict with duties toward individuals, with the interests of a community, with the duties that one has to one's fellow officers, and so on?
3. Discuss examples of immoral laws—laws that have been supported by a majority of people but which (we might argue) should not have been applied by ethical police officers, focusing on higher moral principles.

Utilitarianism

6

> *"The utilitarian doctrine asserts that we should always act so as to produce the greatest possible ratio of good to evil for everyone concerned."*
>
> — J.S. Mill, *Utilitarianism*

Outline

As outlined in chapter 5, doing one's absolute duty is certainly a laudable and defensible way to live much of the time. But such an absolutist approach sometimes ignores the consequences of doing one's duty. The intention-focused approach of Kant has its drawbacks. His idea that the consequences of an act do not factor into the evaluation of the morality of the act largely ignores the actual impact of behavior on the lives of others. Such a focus makes a sort of game out of ethics, a game that is not primarily concerned about the important impact a person's behavior has in the real world. For police officers in particular, such an absolutist, duty-oriented focus is short sighted. The utilitarian school was developed by Jeremy Bentham, and later by John Stuart Mill (its most famous proponent), as a response to these problems. See box 6-1.

6-1 Utilitarianism: Definitions

By the term "utilitarianism" we mean the view that the sole, ultimate standard of right and wrong is the principle of utility. That is, in everything we do we are to seek the greatest possible balance of good over evil in the world. Taking this perspective, when judging what is the right or the wrong thing to do in life, the only criterion to be considered is the good or evil (the consequences) a choice would bring into the world. The final appeal in making ethical choices must be to analyze the comparative amount of good produced by an act or, rather, the comparative balance of good over evil it produces.

Mill was a hedonist in his view about what is good in the sense that he claimed that the moral end of action is the greatest balance of pleasure over pain. But utilitarianism is a theory of obligation that does not entail any particular theory of the good. While a utilitarian must accept the notion that good exists in the world, the lack of a specific definition of what constitutes the good is a drawback of utilitarianism.

Utilitarianism is very democratic in a sense. Utilitarians believe that, in deciding ethical questions, a calculation must be made regarding which choice would maximize the good of the greatest number of people. If we understand utilitarianism this way, the principle tells us we are to distribute good to more people rather than to fewer when we have a choice. The principle of utility thus becomes a double principle, for it tells us: (1) to maximize the balance of good over evil, and (2) to distribute this as widely as possible.

Police officers are faced with duty-related challenges a lot more often than are ordinary citizens because they make so many important decisions in the lives of others and because they moralize for others on a

Box 6-1

Kant Versus Mill—An Example

Suppose a police officer stops a motorist for speeding. Confronting the driver, the officer finds that it is a mother racing to the hospital with a sick child. The officer's knowledge of emergency medicine is such that it is clear the child is in no immediate danger—the young mother is simply overreacting to her child's illness. What should the officer do?

Kant would say the driver was speeding and speeding is illegal. The circumstances, a mother driven by protective fear, are irrelevant. Furthermore, Kant would suggest that the officer could only allow the motorist to proceed without being cited if the officer could will that this be the way in which all such motorists were always treated (a universal law). The implication of such a universal law would be something like this: "One cannot speed unless one thinks there is an emergency situation involved." Because people might define "emergency" in may ways—including being late for a class, for example—strict Kantians would not wish to will such a law. Thus, Kantians would favor the issuance of a citation in the interests of justice.

From Mill's perspective, the police officer should consider the greatest good for the community. This might entail considering (1) that the hysterical mother is not a threat to drive this way all of the time, (2) that other mothers equally situated might very well behave in the same way, (3) that motherhood involves the protection of one's children as a duty that must be taken seriously, and (4) that the long-term best interests of society would be poorly served by issuing such a woman a citation for a moving violation. Thus, Mill might suggest that the officer calm the woman down, explain to her that the child is not in danger, exhort her to drive to the hospital in a more safe manner, and let her go in the interests of justice.

regular basis. Due to the general duties their office imposes upon them, police officers are consistently struggling with such ethical questions as, "Do I do my duty or do I take the easy way out?" Certainly, we would accept the argument (made by Kantians) that the ethical officer, just like the ethical citizen, should always do the dutiful thing. Duty being absolute as it is, our character is determined by how often we stick to doing the right thing, no matter what the cost is to us personally.

Yet what if duty (to the law or to your fellow officers) dictates you do something that is wrong? What if the consequences of doing your own personal duty are that someone else's life is ruined or, at the very least, harmed? What then? (See box 6-2.)

Box 6-2

The Limits of Absolute Duty

In St. Petersburg, Russia, in the fall of 1917, the Russians were losing the war (World War I) to the Germans. Times were terribly hard for the Russian people. Bread riots broke out. People who were literally starving to death took to the streets to protest the sacrifices the war was forcing on them and to demand food for themselves and for their children.

There were so many angry people in the streets that the police could not quell the situation. The government called on the military to help with policing. The Russian Navy, in turn, called on the sailors from the local naval base. These men were ordered to take up their arms and go into the streets to fight against the starving poor people.

The sailors refused. They rejected their duty to the czar, to their country, to the Russian Navy, and to the law. They did this under the threat that they might be shot. Something moved all of these sailors to deny these duties. Something told them that to fight against their own compatriots was not right, that it was not ethical. And history notes this act was one of the reasons the Russian Revolution was born on that day and at that time.

The utilitarians had problems with Kantian absolute duty and thus created their own approach to ethics.

6-1a The Happiness of the Majority

For Kant, happiness was irrelevant to ethics. Ethical principles, the duties related to ethics, were determined logically. They created an absolute system of behavior, and the consequences of that system for individuals or groups of individuals were irrelevant. If doing one's duty was difficult and/or if it did not make a person happy, that had nothing to do with the overall importance of morality being preserved.

The utilitarian school began with the principle that a person should act in a way that would create the greatest happiness for the greatest number of people. When faced with a moral dilemma—a choice between two courses of action, both of which appeared to be ethical—the moral person would calculate the difference in cumulative happiness for the most people and decide which action was best.

For example, if confronted with an arrest/no arrest decision, the police officer following utilitarian principles would consider the long-term implications of each option. If a first-time offender is to be given a warning and let go instead of being arrested, it must be done because the police officer believes that the good of the community ("the greatest number") is being pursued. The logic might be that to arrest a first-time offender would place that person in a situation in jail where he or she would learn from more hardened criminals how to misbehave in still worse ways. This might create more crime in the long run. Or the logic might be that spending too much taxpayer money on a minor offense would be bad.

There are obviously some important and attractive consequences to behaving in this utilitarian way. As we pointed out earlier in this chapter, sometimes doing one's duty can create hardship, pain, and even tragedy. Sometimes, the police keep starving people from food because it doesn't belong to them. Sometimes the police ignore dishonesty by businesses and corporations, actions that hurt large numbers of citizens, because it involves torts and not crimes. Sometimes the police ignore upper-class drug use, upscale prostitution, and white-collar crime and pursue exclusively lower-class offenders because their crime is more visible, because it is easier to pursue to conviction, and because that is what they are told to do by politicians and administrators.

In these and any number of other ways, the police are doing their duties (sticking to the law as written and following their orders in an absolute way). But perhaps in doing so the police participate (indirectly) in perpetuating misery for society's most downcast members. The utilitarian would say that in all of these examples the police should make their own calculations as to what would be the best thing to do. Because a much larger majority of people would benefit from police behaving in a way that is contrary to their apparent duty, the utilitarian would encourage the police to go ahead and ignore the Kantian, absolute devotion to do what is "dutiful." See box 6-3.

For utilitarians, what is "right" is determined in a different way. And as Americans who believe in democracy, we tend to see that the utilitarians do have a good point.

6-1b Individual Happiness

If the happiness of the majority, of the "community" in some sense, is the major focal point of utilitarianism, there is another, more personalized focus upon which calculations about happiness might turn. That is, what of the happiness of the individual? In deciding what action to take

Box 6-3

The Police as Utilitarians

Before the focus on crime control became premiere, the American police, especially in big cities, were general problem solvers and service providers. They performed all sorts of functions that did not fit well into other, existing parts of city administration, such as keeping weather records and being responsible for public health. As one author notes, "Homeless drifters, by the late 1850s, were given nightly lodging in the station houses; by the 1870s, in the bigger cities, tens of thousands of homeless were put up in this fashion annually. In hard times, policemen sometimes ran soup kitchens for the hungry." (Roger Lane, *Policing the City: Boston 1822–1885*, Cambridge, 1967)

Thus, the police officer was considered a combination social worker, public service provider, and community organizer for a long time before the changeover to crime fighter. Is today's call for community-oriented policing just an attempt to bring back some of that service-oriented focus?

---

regarding ethical questions, what if we consider what would be "best" for the individual citizen, for nurturing relationships, or for keeping particular individuals from being hurt?

Instead of focusing on what the consequences might be for the majority of people, utilitarians might also focus on what might be the best course of action for the people involved in an immediate situation. The officer operating in this way might ask, "How should I act to best be of service in the life (lives) of the person(s) involved in the detail I'm now on?" Especially when no obvious law-enforcement-related choices are involved (an arrest/not arrest decision is not being made, for example), an officer might focus on the needs, feelings, and interests of the people with whom he or she is dealing.

For example, what if a homeless person has become a regular "problem" on the beat. Instead of focusing on how to deal with all homeless people or on what laws might be used to incarcerate the individual (ethical formalism), the police officer might decide to take action that would focus on this particular person's needs. Could the officer help this person find a job? Could the officer help to provide this person with immediate relief in the form of food, shelter, counseling, or job training? To do so might be seen as something other than a standard police function. But, given the service role of the police, taking such an individualized form of action is easily rationalized as an appropriate option.

Operating in this manner does not mean that other interests are ignored. Certainly, to solve one homeless person's immediate problem would be in the best interests of the community at large. It would also be in the best interests of justice and crime control (ethical formalism). Thus, several bases can be covered at one time when dealing with the immediate, particularized, personal problems of individual citizens.

The homeless person represents just one commonplace example of how police officers, especially in the age of community based policing, can help individuals in a way that has many positive impacts on the community and on crime fighting. Mentoring individual teenagers to keep them out of gangs and/or away from drugs and crime is another example. Helping elderly people is another example. Police officers can aid the elderly by helping them with their winter heating problems, by referring them to elder-care programs that provide food, by obtaining transportation help from social welfare agencies, and so on. If time permits—that is, if there is time away from crime fighting and order maintenance details— the police can be of service to any number of citizens who are unable to care completely for themselves.

Contemporary police officers have at their disposal all sorts of skills and contacts not enjoyed by society's truly dispossessed. In using these tools to solve individual problems, the police are performing all of their functions at once. And in particular, they are acting as community-oriented problem solvers, as agents of change who use their significant powers in the name of doing good for individuals and for the general populace.

So utilitarianism gives us another set of ideas to ponder. Instead of constructing absolute sets of principles that must be acknowledged and followed at all times and under all circumstances, utilitarianism suggests ethics are situational. Either in focusing on the general good of the community or on the good of the individual citizen, this school underwrites police discretion directly. It suggests that most of the time the police ought to calculate what they think is the best course of action. When making these individualized, particularized, situationally driven decisions, the police use their own logic, pursue their own understandings of the good, and exhibit their character. Thus, an idea that has been flowing through our entire discussion is once more given support: the police are the law, and their personal ethics are critical to the generation of justice. See box 6-4.

Box 6-4

Two Kinds of Utilitarianism

In the world of philosophy, theorists make a differentiation between two types of utilitarianism related to our discussion. "Rule utilitarianism" and "act utilitarianism" involve making Mill's calculations in two different ways.

- **Rule utilitarianism:** Focuses on the good of the entire community/society. It makes calculations of good versus evil that relate to long-term "rules" for all situations that are similar. When faced with an ethical question regarding what to do, rule utilitarians ask, "In the best interests of the majority, what should always be done under the circumstances I am facing?"

- **Act utilitarianism:** Focuses on individual happiness. It makes calculations of good versus evil that relate to the interests of only those immediately involved in a given question. Act utilitarians ask, "What should I do to promote the greatest good and remove the greatest evil for those immediately involved in the decision with which I am faced?"

Note: The strengths and weaknesses of these views are the same—and they are at the heart of this chapter's analysis of what is positive and what is troublesome about the utilitarian view.

Suggesting that the police solve problems one at a time and exercise such a tremendous amount of discretion is not a frustrating reality to the modern professional. Instead, it makes police work an exciting and dynamic profession. It points out that every day on the job is challenging, that every detail may end up going down a different path, and that the individual police officer has a tremendous amount of latitude—and therefore, power—to do good for the community and for individual citizens. In this sense, the utilitarian school presents the most exciting and yet challenging statement of the importance of the role police officers choose to play in society. It makes the most eloquent statement possible about the reason why police work is a rewarding and important calling.

6-2 The Limitations of Utilitarianism

After evaluating the strengths of utilitarianism, we must now consider its drawbacks. If we regard good and bad consequences as the sole criterion of moral worth, we run into several serious problems. See box 6-5.

Box 6-5

Problems Presented by Utilitarianism

- It is difficult to "calculate" amounts of good and evil.
- Merely being good for the majority does not necessarily make an act moral—it ignores the rights of minorities and of individual citizens.
- There is no basis for choosing between equal amounts of good and evil.
- In deterring crime, it does not matter who is punished—the guilty or the innocent.

First, there is the problem of comparing different amounts of good and evil. Consider the famous "lifeboat" example. A lifeboat in a storm-tossed sea is dangerously overloaded and is foundering. To give at least some people a chance of surviving, the first mate decides he must throw a small number of people overboard to make the boat seaworthy, otherwise all will surely die. If he uses a strictly utilitarian reasoning, the first mate must compare the relative good of the larger group of people to the relative evil done to the smaller number.

But how can one possibly do this? Do we really want to say that two lives are "more valuable" than one just because two is a bigger number than one? Is it tolerable for us to imagine that the few should be sacrificed for the sake of the many? And what happened to the idea that a human life is of infinite worth? Attempting to calculate relative goodness and evil is thus a central problem for the utilitarian school.

A second problem is of equal significance. A particular act may be morally right or wrong due to something other than the amount of good over evil it produces. Just because more good for more people might be produced by an act, it might still not be considered moral. Harkening back to the absolutist ideas of Kant, it is easy to criticize the very practical, democratic nature of the logic of Mill. (See box 6-6.) A classic example of how Mill can be criticized involves the institution of slavery.

Suppose that enslaving ten percent of the population, working them day and night, and not paying them for their labors, could produce a better life for the other ninety percent. Then, would a utilitarian conclude slavery is morally right? Sure, ten percent of the people are enslaved—and evil is brought into their lives. But the great majority is afforded a better life—good is brought into their lives. Are we to accept that there are no

Box 6-6

Kant Versus Mill

Kant's ethical formalism emphasizes:

- Consistency in one's maxims where circumstances are ignored
- Reason is the most salient feature of morality
- Focusing on the will/intention behind an act: Kant succeeds in taking people more seriously than Mill

Mill's utilitarianism emphasizes:

- Taking situations into account when deciding what is right
- Calculating what would produce the greatest good for the greatest number of people
- Focusing on consequences; right acts are those which, in their application, promote good over evil, and, thus, Mill takes the good more seriously than Kant.

---

absolute principles (such as, in this case, "slavery is immoral")? Are we to believe that producing more good than evil will define any act as "right"?

A third problem relates to solving ethical dilemmas: choices between equally utilitarian courses of action. One can readily imagine that two possible courses of action, A and B, would produce the same balance of good over evil. Then the utilitarian must say that the acts' "moral scores" are the same. There is no basis for choosing between them. It still may be, however, that they distribute the balance of good in different ways. Action A may give most of the good to a relatively small group of people, while action B may spread the good more equally over a larger segment of the population. In this case, it seems that utilitarians would tell us A is unjust and wrong and B is morally preferable.

For example, a purely utilitarian calculation would rationalize taxing the wealthy at a rate of ninety percent of their earnings and taxing the poor not at all in an effort to maximize overall good. Some people might (and do) support such a taxing policy. But certainly those who have accumulated great wealth as a result of hard work and intelligence would make the argument that to take away the fruits of their labors is immoral. Utilitarianism does not help us with this dilemma.

A fourth criticism—and for police officers perhaps the most troublesome—involves one of the central roles the police play in society, that of deterring criminal activity. Utilitarian logic is always used to rationalize deterrence. Crime is deterred among the majority because a few criminals are caught, imprisoned, and punished for their crimes. In theory, the more certain and harsh the punishment is, the more effective the deterrent impact of the law. The moral rationale for punishing people, and in some cases for punishing them severely, is this utilitarian point about the impact public punishment will have on the great majority. This, for example, is the way in which many people rationalize capital punishment—its application deters others from committing capital crimes.

There is a significant problem with this formula, however. The deterrence effect is created because some people are punished. A critical ethical question for us is: What does it matter if those who are punished are guilty or not? Would not the execution of an innocent person, for example, put just as much fear of the law (perhaps even more) into the minds of those who watched? In accomplishing the desired result of deterring criminal behavior in the general population, those who punish criminals do not have to be particularly careful about whom they punish. As long as some people are punished often enough and severely enough, many others will be deterred from even thinking about deviating.

While the police are not executioners, this point about deterrence is still relevant to police work. The police are often in a position to deter criminality through arrest and the application of force. (The analysis of applying such powers inappropriately will be a major focus in Part 3.) What does it matter if those whom the police arrest and those against whom they use force are actually guilty of being criminals? If the point is to "get the word out" that there will be no toleration of misbehavior on the beat, then the police might just as well arrest and use force on "anyone" as long as it is done in a public fashion so it deters others.

And this dynamic about utilitarianism gives us a tremendous rule of law problem. For the central idea encompassed in the rule of law is that those who are punished deserve it. They are punished if and only if they are guilty of misconduct. No matter how much the rule appliers of the world—in our discussion, the police—may dislike certain people or groups of people (have personal prejudice against them), the rule of law states that such people, if they are not guilty of misconduct, must be left alone.

To punish people for any reason other than that they have behaved in a criminal manner is to create a situation where the police are a law unto themselves. It is certainly possible to argue that such punishment is immoral. Utilitarianism's focus on deterrence suggests this immorality can be overlooked in the name of doing good (deterring criminality) for the majority. This is the height of unfairness to the unjustly punished—it is unethical. It flies in the face of individual constitutional protections that are at the heart of our society's values.

Summary

This much seems clear: An action may maximize the sum of good in the world and yet be unjust in the way in which it distributes this sum. An action that produces a smaller balance of good but does it more justly or fairly may be better. If this is so, then the criterion for determining right and wrong is not merely utility, or maximizing benefit, but also justice. If justice may overrule utility on occasion, then the question of what is right cannot be answered simply in terms of the principle of utility. See box 6-6.

So the happiness of large numbers of people, no matter how much we like the sound of it, might not be the best focal point for creating an ethical perspective. As is true with the absolutist rules and duties of Kant, the utilitarian focus has its strengths and weaknesses. And, as we hope is becoming evident, neither of these two approaches—ethical formalism or utilitarianism—will satisfy all of the needs of all police officers all of the time.

Thus, we turn in chapter 7 to the discussion of a hybrid or combination of these two perspectives created specifically with the police officer in mind. Necessitated by both the drawbacks of these two schools of thought and by the realities of the multiple, conflicting, and vague roles the police must play, we have created for the beat cop "an ethic to live by."

Topics for Discussion

1. Both in box 6-1 and at the end of this chapter, the authors discuss examples of how Kant's and Mill's schools of thought conflict with each other. Discuss examples of police details that illustrate how officers using the two perspectives might react differently and take different action in an effort to behave ethically in the performance of their duties.

2. Consider the lifeboat example given in section 6-2, "The Limitations of Utilitarianism." Assuming you were the first mate and you had decided five people out of twenty had to be thrown overboard to ensure the survival of the remaining fifteen, how would you choose whom to sacrifice? What factors would you take into account and why? Would age, sex, intelligence, education, health, wealth, and so on play a part in deciding who is to live and who is to die?

3. Discuss the implications of the ethical problem presented by the utilitarian logic behind deterrence—that it "doesn't matter who you punish," whether they are guilty or not, it "only matters that you punish someone."

Chapter 7

An Ethic to Live By

> "There is only one question ... When the dust and chips are brushed from a man's life, he will have only the hard, clean questions; did he do well or ill?"
> — From John Steinbeck's *East of Eden*

Outline

We have presented several schools of thought about ethics and discussed several approaches to living a good life. Kant gave us an absolutist perspective. He suggested that duties are fixed and universal and that no amount of rationalization should keep the good person from pursuing the path of righteousness. Furthermore, Kant said that because too much is left to chance, too much is out of our personal control in the world, and our ethics should be judged only by analyzing the intentions we have. The impact of actions in the real world cannot fairly be considered when analyzing personal morality.

The utilitarians gave us another perspective. They suggested not that "rules are meant to be broken" but that life is just too complicated to suggest the long-term impact, the implications of sticking by absolute duties, can be ignored. They wanted us to think about the greater good of the community and/or the good of the individuals immediately involved in a decision when we make ethical choices. They suggested that if cleaving to some absolute duty might do harm to the community or to the individual, then such a duty might very well have to be circumvented.

In chapter 7, we will put together what we have called "an ethic to live by" for the contemporary police professional. This ethic is a hybrid form or combination of these two schools of thought. It includes several important elements of each. After a brief review of why Kant and Mill are too limiting, we will construct a practical, though still very generalized, ethic for the police officer. It will be an ethic that can be applied to day-to-day situations on a regular basis. It is not a "how to do it" guide but rather is a general set of principles from which the professional can view all ethical questions and dilemmas. See box 7-1.

7-1 The Limits of Kant and Mill

We have argued that sensitivity to relevant moral issues is a trait of character that can be cultivated and that this sensitivity is an inherent aspect of moral judgment. Knowing how to see is as much a part of ethical conduct as knowing what to do. What we recognize as the morally relevant features of a situation is a direct indicator of the kind of people we are. For the things that catch our attention determine how we size things up and what we decide to do. The decisions we make are a product of our personal background. It can thus be said that knowing what to do is the natural consequence of knowing how to see. The importance of this fact reminds us that morality is rooted in and grows out of character. When aiming at moral and professional competence, character is the target.

But there remains the moral issue of knowing what to do. If moral principle without good character is powerless, then certainly good char-

Box 7-1

Police Responding to a Higher Duty

On Oct. 4, 2000, in Kolubara, Yugoslavia, thousands of people gathered together to protest. Their concern was that the results of a recently held democratic election were being ignored by their government. The sitting president was refusing to swear in the candidate who had defeated him in the election.

The police were called in to break up the protest, using force if necessary. After a tense confrontation, the police, themselves Yugoslavians, refused to follow orders and use force on their own people. Some took off their police uniforms and went home. One police officer said to an American reporter, "I'm fed up with this. I'm taking my [police] hat and throwing it away. The police [here] are more democratic than you think."

A strict Kantian analysis of this action by hundreds of police officers might conclude these officers had done wrong. They had not stuck by their absolute duty to the government and to obey orders. But our ethic to live by would suggest police officers did the right thing. They refused to do harm to their own people and thus helped to ensure the democratic takeover of the newly elected president. Thus, we are saying this officer had a duty to take off his cap and side with the people.

---

acter without moral principle is blind. In other words, it is not enough to be a morally sensitive person. A good heart is never enough. We must also know how to think. Character governs what we pay attention to, but the importance of good character culminates in knowing what moral principles should direct our judgment. That is the purpose of good character.

Kant denied that people should consider utility (consequence) in determining their ethical perspectives. He said that because no one can control the actions of others, and because no one can know with certainty what the impact of his or her own actions will be, people should do their duty without reference to its consequences. Kant believed that if people attempt to do their duty—as determined by universalizing their intentions—then they are behaving ethically.

But there is a problem here, as we noted in our critique of Kant, for police officers in particular. Taking Kant's view, an act by itself is right or wrong; therefore, the moral quality of the act is determined only by the moral quality of the act. For Kant, the maxim that "a police officer ought to enforce the law" means any police officer who enforces the law is acting ethically—no matter what the consequences. Thus, to cite a speeding motorist who is en route to the hospital with a bleeding gunshot wound is to act morally.

The circular logic of this claim has already been pointed out. The nature of an act, by itself, cannot make it a morally good or bad thing to do. In the above example, citing all speeders to enforce the law at all times may not be morally defensible. Thus, again from chapter 5, the moral worth of an act must depend, at least in part, on something beyond itself, on something about the real difference it makes in the lives of people. We mean that the morality of an act must be directly linked to the good or evil consequences it produces for someone.

So, when we say, "A man is as good as his word"—a Kantian-sounding line—we are really talking about a commitment to others and not just about personal integrity. If people "stick to their word" but the promises they make are to fellow gang members and involve robbing a bank, is it the Kantian conclusion that they are behaving ethically when they rob the bank?

Given these problems with Kant, in combination with others that we have discussed earlier, it would seem that Mill's utilitarianism, with its focus on consequences, would be "the answer" for police officers searching for an ethical perspective. But there are problems with Mill, too. Suppose an action produces far more good than evil. Taking the utilitarian perspective, Mill would say such an action is moral. But it takes us only a moment to think up any number of troublesome examples of this principle in action.

Suppose a police officer decides to shoot a local gang leader or a vicious drug dealer. Wouldn't the evil of committing that murder be outweighed by the good it brought to the community as a whole? Suppose the police beat up every speeding motorist. After a while, wouldn't everyone slow down? And wouldn't driving be much safer? It would be easy to make up a long list of such "practical" evils the police might pursue that are all, on balance, good for the greatest number of community members. (It is a fact of life that in totalitarian states, where the police have the power to do such things, there is very little street crime—the deterrent effect of having vicious, brutal, and unethical police officers is great.)

We realize, therefore, that a particular act may be morally right or wrong because of certain facts about it other than the amount of good or evil it produces. And what we have just said suggests we should recognize two basic principles of obligation: the principle of maximizing good and

Box 7-2

Principle 1 = Beneficence

The obligation to do good and to prevent harm

---

some principle of justice. The resulting ethic would be something like this: we ought always to maximize good in a just way.

This position is Kant-like because (1) right conduct is determined by conforming to a moral principle, and (2) conformity to the principle is an absolute requirement. But our ethic would be much closer to utilitarianism than Kant's own position is because it requires, as fundamental to moral judgment, that we be actively concerned about the good and evil in the world. This, in fact, is our own view, and it is the basis of the theory we will now develop.

7-1a The Principle of Beneficence

The obligation to make people's lives better (including our own) as well as to prevent harm from coming to them suggest this basic principle: One ought to do good and prevent evil. (See box 7-2.)

If people did not have this most basic obligation, we would not be moved to try to bring about as great a balance of good as we possibly can. The police in particular must rise to the challenges of this obligation. Because on the street, on a minute-to-minute basis, they make life-influencing decisions for others, police officers are the individuals in our society who ought to be most directly driven by this obligation.

In other words, in applying the law, in maintaining order, and in providing service to people, the police bear a positive responsibility to do good. They do this by using all of the tools at their disposal to protect the weak from the ruthless, the innocent from the vicious, the young from those adults who would use them as prey, and so on. On the other hand, they bear an equal responsibility to prevent evil. It is not just enough to do good deeds when called upon. That is half of the general charge of the police. They must also work with all the power they possess to prevent evil from occurring and abiding. Taken together, these two duties constitute beneficence. This beneficence principle is a neat and concise statement of what police work is all about. There is no better way to gather together all of the axioms and mottos and platitudes written about police work than this: We should do good and prevent harm.

The reason we call this the principle of beneficence and not the principle of benevolence is to remind ourselves that it asks us actually to do good and not evil, not merely to want to do so. Benevolence means "good will, charitableness, kindliness." To be benevolent is to think well of people and to attempt to act well toward them. It is, in a Kantian sense, intentional—it is all about the general attitude toward others of having good will.

But beneficence means more. Beneficence involves doing good deeds, acting charitably, and behaving in a kindly manner. In other words, beneficence is active and not intentional (concerned merely with a person's intentions). It is not enough, in our discussion of ethics, for police officers to think good thoughts and wish people well. As we said in our criticism of Kant (chapter 6), mere intentions do not "make it" on the street. They are not enough. If it is anything at all, police work is action oriented. The police must engage in doing good and preventing evil. They cannot stand on the sidelines in life and merely have good will. Police officers are umpires or referees, not merely spectators in people's lives.

Our principle of beneficence implies four things (see box 7-3).

First, a police officer ought not to inflict harm on others or do evil. There is an axiom from the physician's code of ethics, the Hippocratic Oath, that says doctors should "first, do no harm." This is a good principle for all professionals to follow. The obvious implications for police officers should not be difficult for us to deduce. In the performance of their duties, police officers must take care at all times to act such that they do not bring more evil (or harm) into a world that is fraught with evil in the first place. When citizens call the police for assistance, they first and foremost ought to be safe in assuming that difficult situations and complicated problems will not be made worse when the police arrive.

Second, a police officer ought take seriously the obligation to prevent evil and harm. For police officers, this means they must be proactive with regard to uncovering evil and alleviating pain and suffering. In an age of community-based policing (CBP), wherein the police are asked to be actively engaged in preventing crime, this admonition stands out as the central idea. Preventing evil and harm before they occur involves a number of strategies. But perhaps most important is the commitment to actively pursue the causes of crime before they have time to fester and grow.

Box 7-3

Implications of the Principle of Beneficence

1. One ought not to inflict evil or harm.
2. One ought to prevent evil or harm.
2. One ought to remove evil.
4. One ought to do or promote good.

Third, a police officer ought to remove evil. The police cannot, must not be anonymous citizens in uniform. They cannot stand on the sidelines and ignore the evil deeds of anyone, especially society's most powerful. To do so would be to abrogate completely the central rationale for having the police in the first place. Society gives a great deal of power to police officers, even allowing them to use lethal force on occasion. The police officers of America ought to be driven by a concern about this power and should always use the power they possess to prevent evil. When officers use force or make arrests, they ought to do so in the name of removing evil and harm from the lives of honest citizens.

Fourth, a police officer ought to promote good. While this seems to be an obvious point, it requires a moment's reflection. No longer driven merely by calls for service but actively operating as agents of change in their communities, the police of today must take seriously their responsibility to do good works. This can involve any number of endeavors, from acting as mentors for troubled youth to taking care of the problems of the homeless to helping elderly citizens with any number of age-related difficulties.

The police of today, under CBP, should do more than look at the crime that happens in the world; they should engage in quality-of-life issues in their communities. CBP involves both sides of the formula underwritten in our principle: The police must be positively engaged with and actively working for their communities both in preventing evil directly and in doing good works.

7-2 The Principle of Distributive Justice: Fairness

Beneficence is important, but not all of our obligations (and decisions) can be derived from the principle of beneficence. This principle does not

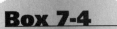

Box 7-4

Principle 2 = Distributive Justice (Fairness)

We ought to make the same relative contribution to the goodness of the lives of others.

---

tell us what is "due" to each person, only that we ought to do good and prevent evil. So the question remains, "What is each person due?" or "What are the rules for the comparative treatment of people?" In other words, how do we distribute justice? (See box 7-4.)

A number of criteria have been proposed over the years in an ongoing discussion of how to distribute resources, status, and justice in a moral society. A central tenet of western liberalism suggests that justice involves dealing with people according to their merits. That is, those who are more worthy receive more. Translated into the world of economics, for example, this principle underwrites the institution of capitalism. People obtain more money (economic wealth) if they work harder, develop better products, provide better services, and so on. Capitalism says that in the business world these people are more worthy than those who are lazy, unproductive, unimaginative, and so forth.

Modern democratic theory is based, in contrast, upon the idea that everyone should receive precisely the same amount of political power. This we do by allowing everyone to cast one vote, and only one vote, in elections. This is called the egalitarian principle of distributive justice (equality in box 7-5).

It simply means that the most fair and just way of distributing political power is to spread it equally among everyone. This may seem to be the only rational way to conduct elections, but it is not. If elections were run with deference to the merit principle, for example, then people's votes might be weighted so that some count for more and some for less; smart, educated or rich people might have their votes count for more than others "because they deserve it." In politics, we have clearly decided in America that the egalitarian principle should prevail.

A third way of distributing justice is related to Karl Marx's principles. Marx was the father of communism who suggested that everyone ought to receive society's benefits according to their needs (*The Communist Manifesto,* Random House, 1932). While most Americans hold some

Box 7-5

Theories of Distributive Justice (or how goods, services, status, and justice should be distributed)

Merit	=	People should receive according to their relative merit.
Equality	=	People should receive exactly equal amounts.
Socialism	=	People should receive according to their need.
Virtue	=	People should receive according to their goodness.

distinctive prejudices about communism, this way of allocating resources, status, and justice is neither evil nor irrational. In fact, all of us are members of small groups that distribute resources and power in this way. These groups are called families. Members receive medical treatment, education, and money not equally but according to their needs. Someone in a family who has special needs, who requires glasses, for example, gets them even if no one else needs them. This way of allocating resources is neither related to merit nor is it equal in its impact.

For our purposes, we will focus on Plato's idea of moral virtue. Plato suggested that we use virtue as a criterion in judging "what each is due" (*The Republic*, Book I). The more virtuous a person is, the more resources he or she receives. This, too, is a morally defensible method of allocation. It says that those who behave themselves are rewarded in ways that those who do not behave are not. It says that those who work harder get more. It says that those who are smarter receive deference for their intelligence, and so on.

As one can readily see, Plato's idea includes within it the principle of merit. But merit, as historically applied by other philosophers, can include social standing or class. A person can receive more because of his or her position in society and not just because his or her actions are more virtuous. Thus, the virtue principle goes further than merit. It suggests that people who behave in a virtuous manner, by being hardworking, intelligent, and educated (with which the merit principle agrees) are joined by those who show compassion, kindness, and empathy. All of these are considered important virtues, and anyone who is virtuous must receive "credit" for being so in terms of the distribution of justice.

Now, we can only use virtue as the principle upon which to decide the distribution of justice if each individual has an equal chance to develop virtues as much as he or she is capable. Life deals with each of us differently. What about the beaten and abandoned child? What about the Vietnam veteran with serious injuries? Before virtue can be adopted as our standard for resource distribution, we must all have had the same chance to achieve it.

Therefore, we suggest that we ought to modify Plato's position to say that our second criterion of morality shall be: "We ought to do what we can to give each person the same conditions for achieving virtue." And thus, justice means making the same relative contribution to the goodness of people's lives—namely that they be supported in "making the most of themselves."

How does this relate to police work? Certainly, the police cannot be expected, even in the CBP era, to right all of the wrongs that have been done to people. The police cannot reconstitute the major institutions of society so they are equitable and fair. We do not and cannot suggest this. But what we can suggest is that police officers focus on the theoretical discussion here and apply its principles to the things on the street they can control. This means the enlightened, competent, ethical officer needs to think about several things at once.

First, it is important to understand that treating people fairly does not mean treating them identically. Because of their circumstances, strengths, weaknesses, abilities, and so on, people might be treated in different ways by the police but still be treated "fairly." In other words, treatment that takes life's variables into account might mean different treatment for different people, but it also means if citizens were equally situated in life (had the same opportunities, education, abilities, and so on) then they might be treated in exactly the same way.

This might sound confusing, so an example is in order. In the interests of justice, a police officer might cite one motorist for double-parking and allow another to go uncited because he or she was in a great hurry taking a child to a hospital emergency room. Both motorists might be equally guilty of causing a traffic problem, and the egalitarian principle of justice might require that precisely the same action be taken in both cases. But in the hospital-related example, the motorist is allowed to move the car later, without penalty, due to the circumstances involved. In such an example, both motorists were treated fairly (given their different circumstances) and equitably (they both would have received leniency if they both had a medical emergency), but they were not treated identically.

Box 7-6

Distributing Justice Fairly

We have noted that penalties, such as fines for speeding, impact people in unequal ways. This reality is being changed in some European countries through the imposition of what are called "day fines." When people are fined for minor infractions, they are fined the equivalent of one or two (etc.) days worth of wages. Thus, a day fine meted out for the crime of drunk driving of "five days" might cost a doctor $5,000, a teacher $1,000, and someone living at the poverty level $250. Arguably, this practice hits everyone fined in an equally forceful way. This is an example of how some countries are wrestling with the idea of how to distribute justice fairly.

Second, our concept of justice does not mean the actions of the police will make people's lives equally good. A decision not to arrest one person may make only a marginal difference in his or her life. The same decision granted to another may make a tremendous difference. Consider, for example, that avoiding a speeding fine of $150 might have little impact on a rich person's life but could make a great impact on that of a poor person. The police cannot control this reality. It is but one example of life's unfairness that is out of the hands of uniformed police officers.

Thus, the police must use their discretionary decision-making powers to further the interests of justice in a way that attempts to treat everyone fairly. But we can neither assume that such treatment will always be exactly the same nor that it will impact people's lives in a similar way. See box 7-6.

We have argued here that justice is not driven by, nor is it independent of, the principle of maximizing benefit (the principle of utilitarianism). But justice is driven by the principle that we ought always to promote the good because we understand justice as the principle that we ought to make the same relative contribution to the goodness of people's lives. Justice is the principle that implements the good, and without justice, the principle of promoting the good cannot live. The existence of justice is inescapably necessary for the realistic possibility of promoting and maintaining goodness in people's lives.

Summary

The basic idea of our argument is that (1) our single, most dominant moral obligation is to care about and promote goodness where we can, and (2) this obligation requires the further principle of justice, now identified as equal treatment. The first principle asks us to be actively concerned about the goodness and evil of people's lives, while the second asks us to be fair in the way we deal with people.

The principle that we ought to promote the good constitutes an absolute and universal requirement, and there is no other principle as fundamental to the idea of an ethical life as this one. It is absolute because there can be no exceptions and universal because it applies to everybody. From this one principle springs every moral duty we have. The principle of justice is responsive to the principle of promoting the good and is understood as the implementation of it. Therefore, without our first principle, justice has no meaning; but without justice, promotion of the good and prevention of evil is impossible.

Must we recognize any other principles of right and wrong? It seems to us that we need not. As far as we can see, all of the things we may wish to recognize as moral duties (kindness, honesty, courage, etc.) and all our judgments about what to do in specific situations originate in these two principles, either directly or indirectly. From the first principle follow various specific rules of *prima facie* (at first view) obligation, for example those of not injuring anyone and of not interfering with another's liberty. From the second principle follow others, like equality of consideration and equality before the law. Some—like telling the truth, not being cruel or not tormenting animals—may follow separately from both principles. Others—like keeping promises and taking care of one's children—may be justified on the basis of the two principles jointly.

We began our discussion about moral judgment by arguing that the concepts of "the good" and "justice" can be understood as the chief organizing principles of human life and that they emerge directly and necessarily from the most fundamental kinds of human experience. Our "ethic to live by" is a fusion of these two principles. We determine what to do in this or that situation by consulting the usual moral rules we are familiar with (be loyal, don't gossip, be kind, etc.). But our discussion has shown that the way to tell what moral rules to live by in specific situations is to see which rules best fulfill the joint requirement of promoting the good and justice.

We are constantly being "questioned" by life, by the world, with regard to whether or not we are living a good, ethical life. But being asked to live this way has the force of an imperative, for we really have no choice but to heed the request. That is, we have no choice if we want to be found worthy, if we want to live a decent life, if we want to do competent work. The profession of policing guarantees nobody is questioned in this way more than the police officer. Police officers' responses depend on nothing as much as how they see themselves, and this is entirely a matter of character.

Topics for Discussion

1. In an effort to better understand the principle of beneficence, consider this idea of promoting good and preventing evil. Discuss examples from everyday life of how people might behave so as to follow this rule. Then discuss police-related examples of how one might apply beneficence on the job.

2. Refer to box 7-5. Discuss examples from everyday life in which each of these different methods of distributing justice might be considered morally defensible.

3. Police officers attempting to promote justice cannot undo all of the unfairness and inequality in the world. But what can they do? In the CBP era, what types of actions can police officers take on the job that might have a positive impact on the lives of citizens who are the most needy in our society? In other words, how do police officers behave in today's world as "agents of change"?

Judgment Calls

> "When I serve alcohol, they call it bootlegging. When the mayor serves it on Lakeshore Drive, they call it hospitality."
> — Al Capone

Outline

Was Al Capone, the infamous criminal, correct in the quote above? Are there inconsistencies in the application of the law in America? Are some laws applied to some people and not to others? Were some laws intended to impact some people and not others? Are there laws that are so vague it is hard to understand them much less apply them in a fair manner? Are there occasions where different laws even conflict with each other? The answer to all of these questions, of course, is yes. And because all of these problems are real and complicate the application of the rule of law on the street, the job of being a police officer is extremely difficult from a legal perspective.

In chapter 8, we will explore the frustrating fact that police officers must make judgment calls on a regular basis. Reflecting on the problem that laws can be multiple, conflicting, and vague, we must remind ourselves of the fact that the police also have multiple, conflicting, and vague roles to play. In this discussion, we will relate these realities to our ethic to live by.

8-1 When Beneficence Conflicts with Justice

As noted throughout this text, police work is complicated by the fact that police play multiple, conflicting, and vague roles in American society. Law enforcement, order maintenance, and service are the general headings under which these multiple roles fall. In chapters 5, 6 and 7, we engaged the idea that many ethical perspectives are relevant to police work. Our ethic to live by has been created in an attempt to make sense of the conflict that Kant's and Mill's ethical perspectives create for the police.

When the police are making arrest/no arrest decisions, they are performing their law enforcement duties. The decisions they make must be based on solid, irrefutable criteria. A person is only arrested if there is probable cause to believe he or she has committed a crime. There must be specific evidence to show this. The elements of the crime must be present. There must also be specific evidence to show this. In a country that respects the rule of law, these are absolute requirements. The right of *habeas corpus,* written into our constitution, puts these requirements about legal specificity into one of our most basic legal principles: A person has to be charged with a particular crime or be set free.

This seems to mean that police officers who perform the role of law enforcement officers are Kantians. They must be absolutists because they are dealing with people's freedom. When they decide to take away that freedom or to leave it be, police officers must apply absolute legal principles, procedural rules, and substantive laws. As we noted in the introduction to this book, the rule of law demands that no amount of personal bias on the part of a police officer about a person's behavior can substitute for the breaking of specific laws. If laws are not broken, then the person goes free.

Similarly, it seems when police officers are operating in the order maintenance mode, they often use a utilitarian frame of reference. When maintaining order and not dealing with law-enforcement-oriented decisions, police officers spend their time calculating what is in the best interests of the state and of all the people. When dealing with drunks, the homeless, parties, loud music, groups of juveniles, family troubles, and a host of other order-maintenance types of details, the police consistently calculate what to do with an eye toward what they understand to be fair and equitable in the local community. In this way, the police balance conflicting interests and act in a very democratic fashion, attempting to make decisions that benefit the greatest number of people.

Then there is the service role of the police. In this context, police officers also tend to make utilitarian-type decisions. Neither reflecting on the long-term interests of justice in the state (law enforcement/Kantian decisions) nor fairness and equitability in the local neighborhood (order maintenance/rule utilitarian decisions), service orientation demands something different. It requires that police officers consider the best interests of just those people immediately involved in a given detail. They are not making calculations about the good of the community or of the greatest number of people.

Because of the confusion between these types of ethical perspectives brought out by the multiple, conflicting, and vague nature of the police officer role, we have created our ethic to live by. But even in applying that ethical perspective, the police are sometimes confronted with judgment calls. One kind of judgment call occurs when beneficence conflicts with justice. See box 8-1.

When justice (again, defined as fairness) conflicts with beneficence, the latter becomes paramount. This might put the police officer in a bind sometimes, but dealing with such binds (by making discretionary decisions) is a central reality of police work. Standing up for what is ethical and doing the right thing under such circumstances are actions the officer with good character takes and embraces willingly.

Dealing with the bind created when justice conflicts with beneficence involves understanding something that we addressed in our discussion of justice in chapter 7. That is, treating people fairly does not mean treating them exactly the same way. Remember our example, from chapter 7, of the two motorists who are double-parked in front of a hospital? One raced there with a bleeding victim in tow, the other doubled-parked sim-

Box 8-1

Beneficence Conflicting with Justice

What happens when, in doing good and removing harm, the police are confronted with the reality that they cannot promote justice or fairness? For example, justice may dictate the arrest of a 12-year-old burglar, in fairness to all burglars and in fairness to all burglary victims. The question may become, can this duty to justice be overridden by the utilitarian idea that the age and lack of criminal record of the child dictates another course of action? Is the duty to behave in a beneficent manner controlling? We think that it is. Beneficence is paramount, and this is a principle that must be included within an understanding of our ethic to live by.

ply out of convenience. We are saying in this section that doing good for those people may very well involve treating them differently. As long as competent, ethical officers understand in their hearts that they would treat other citizens in the same manner, then our ethic does not require equal treatment.

In other words, ethical officers must be comfortable with the idea that all people who double-park at hospitals because of genuine emergencies should be let off with a warning. Equally, ethical officers must know in their hearts that all people who double-park out of laziness should be cited. As long as such decisions are made irrespective of race, color, creed, class and so on (characteristics that are morally irrelevant to the issue at hand), the competent, professional, ethical officer can be comfortable with such inequitable treatment. While in a pure sense such actions (citing one and not citing the other) are not "just," they are beneficent. And beneficence is the controlling principle.

8-2 The Harm Principle: What's a Legal Problem?

All societies must strike a delicate balance when they decide how much power the agents of the state should possess. A classical liberal, such as John Locke (who gave us the idea of natural rights and limited government), would say that individuals should be left alone to live their own lives without interference from the state or government. (See Peter Laslett, ed., Locke's *Two Treatises of Government,* New York, 1960.) A classical conservative, such as Edmund Burke (who led the opposition to Locke's ideas in England three hundred years ago), would say people cannot be trusted with their own decisions. Burke would, and did in his day, call for strong government, tight laws, and increased police powers. He believed that the people, being ignorant and stupid, needed to be controlled using any means possible. (See Charles Parkin, *The Moral Basis of Burke's Political Thought*, New York, 1956.)

In America, we have our own "classical" statement of the trade-off between the power of the state and the freedom of the individual, and it comes (again) from John Stuart Mill. In his famous essay "On Liberty," Mill suggested a formula for how much power belonged in whose hands. Mill said the individual should only be amenable to society for that conduct which directly harms another. This is called Mill's "harm principle," and it is important for all police officers to remember. See box 8-2.

The harm principle is important because it provides a good yardstick for making judgment calls. That is, often police officers must decide whether or not to invoke the law, whether or not to arrest, and/or whether or not to become involved in solving problems that might otherwise be solved if people were simply left alone. When this occurs, it serves the police well to remember Mill and to ask themselves whether or not someone is directly harmed by the actions of another. In other words, if there is no direct harm to others from deviant behavior, why worry about it?

For example, if loud music is coming from a rowdy party but there have been no complaints to the police about it, who cares? Or if a pair of backpackers decides to make love in the forest and no one sees them but a police officer, who cares? Or if teenagers are out after curfew on their way home from a school function that ran a little late and are minding their own business, who cares? Or if married couples are turned on by the idea of swapping partners for sexual liaisons in the privacy of their own homes and bedrooms, who cares? In these and a thousand other instances, people might break the law and/or behave deviantly but not create the sort of problem that one might think ought to be "the business" of the state or of the police. See box 8-3.

Now Americans have a long tradition of believing in Mill's philosophy about personal harm and about keeping the government out of our lives. And this discussion of Mill brings up two important additional points for police officers. First, the competent professional, understanding Mill and the American ideals of limited government and individual rights, must avoid the tendency to feel frustrated when this ideal is put into action. That is, one of the overt manifestations of Americans' agreement with Mill and their belief in the principle of limiting governmental power is their propensity to be suspicious of the police and of police power. The intelligent police officer understands this and makes allowances for people's very natural "American-like" behavior in (often) distrusting the police.

Box 8-2

Mill and the Power of the State

John Stuart Mill suggested three main reasons why decisions relating to people's personal lives (where no direct harm to others could result from the outcome) should be left in the hands of individuals and not given over to the power of the state or government.

- Usually, people know better than bureaucrats, politicians, or police officers how best to decide questions about their own lives because of their intimate knowledge of their own interests, goals, desires, and so on.

- On those occasions wherein government agents know better what is good for the citizen than people do themselves, it is still usually best to leave decisions to individuals. Even though people may make mistakes, part of our intellectual development and maturation in life is learning through trial and error.

- Given the universal propensity of governmental power over the individual to expand, we should always remain reluctant to create more governmental structures—they will almost invariably endure and, in the long run, lessen individual freedom.

Second, while we may all applaud the harm principle and believe the state and the police should keep out of people's lives whenever possible, one dynamic in contemporary American society stands in the way of applying this ideal. As one might imagine, when people analyze the concept of "victimless crimes," crimes for which there are no specific, individual complainants, Mill's philosophy is always in the forefront of discussion. See box 8-3. This is because victimless crimes involve no direct harm to others. And a remarkable number of Americans agree in leaving victimless crime alone. Studies indicate, for example, that large numbers of people believe citizens should be left alone if they are gambling, reading "smut," viewing pornography, or enjoying consensual adult sexual behavior in their own homes.

One of the classic victimless crimes is drug use. And given the monumental effort being undertaken in America and throughout the world in the name of the "drug war," the application of the harm principle to drug use is a major stumbling block for the police. Estimates of the numbers of Americans who have used illegal drugs range above the seventy million

Box 8-3

The Characteristics of Victimless Crimes

- Consenting participants on both sides of the criminal act (such as prostitute and "John," gambling partners, illicit sexual partners)
- An ongoing demand for the goods/services that are provided
- Significant amounts of official corruption due to high profits and the absence of witnesses/complaining parties when officials (usually the police) interact with criminals

---

mark. Furthermore, any number of studies indicates that about twelve percent of the population—regardless of socio-economic level, race, or class—use illicit drugs. Thus, a huge number of Americans, not merely those who use crack and heroine in the inner cities, create the demand for illegal drugs on an ongoing basis.

This creates several problems for the police. First, such black market profits tend to create corruption because officials, police officers included, can be "bought off" by drug dealers who possess incredible amounts of money. For the purposes of our discussion of police ethics, the drug war creates a black market that almost invariably seduces some police officers into lives of crime.

Second, and more relevant to our discussion here, because drug use does not directly harm anyone other than the user, the involvement of the police in the drug war creates a philosophical problem relative to Mill's concerns about personal freedom. Many people resent the injection of the state's power into the lives of citizens unless the lives and property of others are in jeopardy. Gambling, prostitution, and alcohol-related crimes are all examples of the sorts of criminal behaviors wherein the police operate along a sliding scale. Obvious, flagrant, public violations, especially when someone complains about them, are often prosecuted. But consensual, adult, private violations can be, and in most jurisdictions usually are, ignored.

For practical reasons, we have to put drug use aside and keep it off this list. The individual police officer, no matter how sensitive he or she might be to the paradoxes of the drug war, can hardly be expected to stand in the way of such a large-scale endeavor. It is true that a steadily increasing number of citizens, analysts, politicians, and even police officers have become opposed to this war. But a majority of Americans, a majority of police officers, and certainly a huge majority of police administrators are still in favor of its prosecution. Thus, given that the police are supposed to be accountable to public opinion, the law, and their departments' orders (see chapter 1), we must keep drug use separate from this discussion of the harm principle and other victimless crimes.

"A good referee should try to be invisible whenever possible. He shouldn't control or even be a part of the game, if it isn't absolutely necessary. He should just let 'em play football."

— John Madden, Football Coach

Thus, our discussion of the harm principle must carry a "drug war asterisk" next to it. But generally, aside from the realities of fighting the drug war, Mill's harm principles translates into police work in this way: Police officers ought to leave people alone, not take official action, as often as possible—when no one else is directly harmed. With the exception of felonious crime and, of course, violent crime, police officers, like "good referees," should try to be invisible. Barring violence, felony crime, or direct harm to others, police officers ought to be a part of life's scenery.

8-3 Solving Ethical Dilemmas

We often hear that people show their character when they are faced with ethical questions. In life we are sometimes faced with a choice between doing the right thing and doing the easy thing or the safe thing or the comfortable thing or the hedonistic ("feel good") thing. People show what they are really made of when they decide how they will behave under such circumstances. Life presents everyone with such questions on a regular basis. Do I pad my tax returns with false deductions or tell the truth? Do I stick to my marriage vows or pursue the good-looking co-worker? Do I lie to my kids about my drug use when I was a kid or do I "come clean"? In this way, life presents everyone with large and small ethical choices to make that involve balancing the right thing to do against the easy thing to do.

But things get more complicated than this. Life also presents us with ethical dilemmas: choices between conflicting duties. An ethical question may be hard to answer. But when one does the right thing in facing an ethical question, even though it might be difficult, one is left with a good feeling about oneself. When a person tells the truth, cleaves to his or her spouse, acts loyally, behaves like a good parent, and so on, that person gets the satisfaction of knowing that his or her good character is being exhibited.

But what happens when you have to decide between two courses of action, each of which has a good, solid, ethical duty attached to it? What happens when a genuine ethical dilemma presents itself? Police officers, more than most people, are faced with such decision making because they so often have to decide between the conflicting claims of diverse people. Often on the street, both sides in a dispute are right, both sides are arguing from perfectly reasonable perspectives, and both sides are making moral claims that are defensible. What does the police officer do when confronted with such dilemmas? See box 8-4.

Criminal ethicist Joycelyn Pollock attempts to help the individual decision maker (in our discussion the police officer) with such evaluations. After reading such a list (box 8-4), one might be frustrated that it does not give a specific explanation about how to solve such dilemmas. But the complicated nature of life on the street dictates that thoughtful analysts and experienced practitioners will only be able to provide us with such general sets of guidelines as these. Because there are millions of sets of facts, sets of circumstances, and sets of participants in the world, the competent police officer can only be given approaches and cannot be shown all solutions for dealing with real-life dilemmas.

So Pollock tells us, in essence, to be as careful and thoughtful and thorough as we can, given the pressures of time on the beat. Make sure the facts are clear. Make sure assumptions, prejudices, and predictions are left out of decision making. Be clear what the relevant interests are, what ethical duties present themselves to all parties, and what constitute the most immediate ethical issues.

Consider this example. Suppose you are on a detail where a husband has been accused of abusing his wife. The accusation comes from her mother, the grandmother of the children who stand around you as you survey the situation in the family's living room. The wife looks shocked and exhausted—as if she might very well have been attacked by her husband. On the other hand, she has no wounds showing, no blood flowing, no visible trauma. She says that he did not assault her. She is obviously afraid of the man but is adamant that he should be left alone.

The grandmother is equally adamant about having seen an assault, about the need for the police to take the man to jail, and about her duty

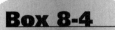

Box 8-4

Pollock's Analytical Steps to Clarifying Ethical Dilemmas

While there is not "one way" to decide between conflicting ethical duties when making behavior choices, criminal ethicist Joycelyn Pollock suggests several steps be taken by individuals who seek to clarify an ethical dilemma. Her steps are:

- Review all the facts—not future predictions, not suppositions, not probabilities, but what is known.

- Identify all the potential values of each party that might be relevant—life, law, family, and self-preservation.

- Identify all possible moral issues for each party involved.

- Decide what is the most immediate moral or ethical issue facing each individual.

- Resolve the ethical dilemma. Make an ethical judgment based on an appropriate ethical system (e.g., our ethic to live by) and supported by moral rules (such as "one must always follow the law").

(Joycelyn Pollock, *Ethics in Crime and Justice,* 3rd ed. Belmont, Calif., 1998

to protect her daughter and grandchildren. What do you do? There is, of course, no single answer to this question. The physical state of the people involved would need to be assessed. Are they drunk? Drinking? Using drugs? The history of the family would have to be taken into account. Have you been there before? Has the husband been arrested for abuse before? Has the wife herself complained before? What is the relationship of the grandmother to the family? Is she in the home on a regular basis? Has she complained before? Do you, the officer on the scene, believe that she means well and truly wants to protect her daughter and grandchildren? Or is she trying to break up a marriage for her own reasons?

These and a dozen other variables need to be taken into consideration. When you do this, considering Pollock's chart can be helpful. Rather than swimming in all of these details and rather than making an intuitive decision that might be ineffectual, the competent professional will attempt to analyze the problem logically. The ethical duties of the mother, father, and grandmother, not to mention those of the police, must be considered.

The duty to protect people from abuse (removing evil) must be considered and weighed against the duty to keep the family unit together (promoting good). Using our ethic to live by, the police officer may not see an apparent solution, one that answers the "what to do" question in a precise manner. While we believe our ethic is an important compromise between other schools of thought, we cannot argue that it "solves" all such dilemmas in a concrete way.

For who, in the middle of a hot detail and under the pressure of time and multiple stressors, has the time to write all of this down and do such calculating? The answer, of course, is that no one does. But we (and Pollock) are not suggesting that officers do so. We (and she) are suggesting that in training sessions, in informal discussions, in reviewing how past details have been handled, and so on, competent police officers can and should go over these types of options when they have the time to do so. If they do, their competence, as a function of their effectiveness in dealing with ethical dilemmas, will grow.

This is just one common example of a type of ethical dilemma presented to the officer on the beat. Viewed relative to appropriate ethical perspectives and related to moral rules that make up the officer's understanding of the good life and of the important elements of community, such dilemmas need not present police officers with frustration. Understanding that theirs is a limited role, that they cannot solve all the world's problems, police officers who approach such problems and make judgments based on these principles will more often than not be acting as competent professionals.

8-4 The Police Officer's Craft

Long ago, sociologist Jerome Skolnick wrote a book suggesting police work was something between a blue-collar trade type of job and a white-collar professional type of job (*Justice Without Trial*, New York, 1967). He likened police work to a "craft." He suggested that the combination of academic knowledge, street sense, particularized skills, and intuitive logic cops needed to possess made their occupation something like that of the fine craftsman.

Today, we are suggesting this definition be amplified, pushed one step further. For when the increasingly complex set of knowledge and skills (the craft) is modified and applied through a screen that puts the entire job into an ethical frame of reference, police work becomes a genuine profession. Making the types of judgment calls we have discussed in chapter 8 is the essence of the professional's role in this modern era. And it is driven, as we have said numerous times, by individual police officer character.

Summary

In this chapter, we have reflected directly upon both the frustration and the positive nature of police discretionary decision making. Our ethic to live by is, we believe, presents for the police practitioner a good set of principles upon which to depend when approaching the types of problems that police officers regularly encounter on the street. Nevertheless, it is not a practical "how to solve all types of details" set of rules. No such list can be created for all of the complicated and challenging problems presented to police officers.

In fact, no such list should even be attempted. This is because human behavior and human interactions are so complex and diverse, and the stresses of police work are so great, that any such attempt would fall prey to two problems at once. First, such a list would invariably be incomplete. The practitioner is thus better served by such general guidelines as we have provided. Second, this type of list would tend to imply to officers that there is "one way" to solve specific types of details. The complexity of police work, amplified by the time constraints imposed by real life, is just so great that this is not the case. The ethical dilemmas that are consistently a part of the job must be approached with our ethic as a set of guiding principles, and not as an absolute formula for success in decision making.

Thus, here in chapter 8 we have engaged the idea that judgment calls must be tempered by several understandings. First, beneficence can conflict with justice. Wen that happens, for reasons that we have above considered, beneficence must be the controlling principle. Second, police officers must remember Mill's harm principle at all times. They must weigh it constantly, especially when deciding whether or not to take action at all. Whenever possible, "no harm, no foul" should be a guiding light for the competent officer on the street.

We now turn in Part 3 to a set of more practical discussions about specific types of police misconduct.

Topics for Discussion

1. Discuss the idea that the two parts of our ethic to live by, beneficence and justice, can conflict. Consider examples from police work where they do conflict and discuss why beneficence must be the controlling principle.
2. Discuss victimless crimes. What are examples and what are the elements they all have in common? With an eye toward Part 3's discussion of particular types of police misconduct, consider why victimless crimes almost invariably produce police corruption.
3. Discuss the difference between an ethical question and an ethical dilemma. First, consider examples from life in general. Then discuss examples from police work.

Applications

Having discussed the importance of individual police officer character, having reviewed several classic schools of thought about ethics, and having developed our own ethic to live by for the modern police professional, it is now time to apply these concepts to the work-a-day world of the police officer. In Part 3, we will get more practical, take a more "nuts and bolts" focus, and discuss specific types of police misconduct and how our ethic applies to them.

First, in chapter 9 we will present a typology that differentiates between the five different types of misconduct into which police officers sometimes fall. Then, in chapters 10, 11 and 12 we will focus directly on the different types of misconduct, their causes, and how the ethical professional, individually and as a member of the police subculture and a given police organization, can and should approach the sometimes daunting task of avoiding such behavior.

Types of Police Misconduct

> *"Power corrupts. Absolute power corrupts absolutely."*
> — Lord Acton

Outline

It is always uncomfortable for police officers and those who would be police officers to confront the topic of police misconduct. We know how hard it is to be a cop on the beat. We understand the stresses and violence involved. We are confident that the overwhelming majority of police officers do the very best job they can against the odds. Thus, we tend to want to shy away from this negative subject.

But no amount of avoidance will change the reality that police officers, like people in any other line of work, are sometimes guilty of misbehaving. The power the police possess is great. They are licensed by society to take away people's freedom, to use force, and even to use deadly force. It is perhaps more important for police officers of America to "behave themselves" than it is for any other political, social, economic, or legal actors to do so.

In chapter 9, we will discuss the various types of police misconduct into which police officers sometimes fall. We will take time to understand the differences between these types and to outline for chapters 10, 11 and 12 the characteristics that define police deviance in a way that makes our discussions of police ethics more clear and focused.

9-1 Standards of Conduct

Police officers are sometimes guilty of "deviance" in the same way and for the same reasons citizens are guilty of deviance. Greed, opportunity, chance, necessity, and conscious decisions based on poor moral judgment all contribute to police deviance. This is not a book about the causes of deviance in the police world, so we will merely remind ourselves here that there are numerous causes and complicated patterns of behavior that lead to such misconduct.

But we do need to explore briefly what is meant by "deviance." When people deviate, they break norms of conduct that are prescribed for them. Norms can be defined as cultural values, moral tenets, social customs, or codified laws. Of course, people (and police officers) can break any number of norms and behave in deviant ways without becoming the subject of anything other than disapproval. If people pick their noses in public or talk too loudly in theaters or say bad things about a dead person, they may make us think ill of them. By doing these and countless other things, they may invite people to think they are ignorant, stupid, rude, insensitive, and so forth. Such disapproval is powerful stuff and makes most of us behave in the ways that we do. That is, to avoid social disapproval we dress, talk, and act the way we do most of the time.

Box 9-1

Multiple Standards of Conduct

- Police officers are legal actors.
- Police officers are political actors.
- Police officers are administrative actors.

But such deviance is only informally sanctioned. Sometimes people transgress distinctive, written rules of conduct. When they do this, they are subjected to the operations of the institutionalized systems that are society's official behavior-control mechanisms. When people break the law, they may be arrested, jailed, tried, convicted, and punished. Similarly, when a cop breaks the rules of conduct set up for the police, he or she may be accused, investigated, found guilty, and punished. In the case of citizens, the criminal justice system does the work of holding them accountable. In the case of the police, police review systems, internal affairs units, or civilian review boards do the work.

Police review systems can, therefore, be considered mini criminal-justice systems. They investigate allegations of misconduct and make findings about the guilt of accused officers. These systems come in all shapes and sizes. They have a thankless job to do in attempting to hold the police accountable for their actions. For just like the criminal justice system itself, police review systems operate after the fact. That is, they deal with accusations of misconduct after they have happened. Our task here is to talk about internalizing standards of ethical conduct so police officers do not break the rules in the first place. We are, therefore, making the point that internalized ethics are more important than prescribed rules. The institutions of the family, schools, churches, clubs, and so on attempt to internalize standards of behavior, and so does this book.

But this begs us to ask, what standards are we talking about? Where are the standards of conduct to which the police must be held accountable? As was true earlier in our discussion of the roles of the police, the standards to which we hold the police are multiple, conflicting, and vague. Thus, as was true of police roles, there will always be some confusion about where we should find the yardstick to evaluate police behavior. See box 9-1.

9-1a Cops As Legal Actors

The police have three separate sets of standards to which they must look for guidance. First, and some would say foremost, the police must answer to the law. Everything a police officer does must be legal. When applying codes and statutes, police officers must be legally correct in their decisions. They must know the codified law, charge appropriately, investigate effectively, and write reports that are legally tight and include the appropriate elements.

On the other hand, when dealing with citizens and suspects the police must also know case law. They must treat citizens with deference to the constitutionally prescribed rights all Americans possess. They must know under what circumstances they can stop and field interrogate people, how and when to admonish suspects of their rights, when they can and cannot make warrantless searches, and so on. Here, too, the police must be legally precise. They must intelligently apply the rule of law in a professional manner.

9-1b Cops As Political Actors

However, the law represents only one set of standards for the police. A second set of standards comes from the constituents in the communities they serve. If the police must be legal actors in sticking to the dictates of the law, they must equally be political actors in responding to the desires of their communities. They are "street-corner politicians," as author William K. Muir labeled them (see chapter 1). In today's era of community-based policing, the police are asked to form bonds with the community, to encourage neighborhood groups to inform them of their desires, and to behave in a responsive manner, taking such feedback into account when they police the streets. Especially under these circumstances, the police must be held accountable to standards of conduct prescribed by the people.

This may sound easy. To answer to the law as legal actors and to answer to the people as political actors may seem perfectly proper and logical. But trouble can arise when these two sets of standards conflict. When the people ask the police to do things that are not legal, as they do more often than one might think, there is a distinctive conflict between these two sets of standards (see box 9-2). People will regularly ask the police to do whatever it takes to get rid of drugs on the streets, to break up local gangs, to curb domestic abuse, to protect children from guns, and so forth. Not being police officers, and not caring (really) about what the law says, people on the street expect the police to take effective action against these evils and to do it without delay.

Box 9-2

Asking the Police to Do the Impossible

When doing research into gang-related crime in the inner city in Kansas City, Mo., one of the authors interviewed a woman who lived in the heart of gang country. The woman said, "I'll tell you where the drug houses are. Why don't you come down in the middle of the night and burn them down? We'll all stand behind you!"

This example illustrates how the police are often put into a strange place. We know this woman meant well and that she was probably right about the law-abiding citizens of the neighborhood standing behind the police if they literally burned the drug dealers out of town. Furthermore, such tactics as burning down a crack house may in fact "work" to get the dealers to leave the area—it is a practical solution, in other words. But such solutions are obviously far from legal.

What are the police to do in a society that experiences increased fear from violence, gangs, drugs, and guns—and where it could easily be argued that a majority of law-abiding citizens would, in fact, want the police to do whatever it takes to get the job done?

Because it is not clear how to resolve such conflicts, the police and any system that attempts to hold them accountable for their actions are put in a bind. Should the police harass people whom they know to be drug dealers or gang members, whether or not they are observing the Constitution? Should the police target known drug dealers for special treatment even though there is no legal evidence against them? Should an individual police officer threaten to "personally kick the crap out of you" to deter a wife beater from doing it again? All of these tactics are, arguably, effective in doing things a majority of the people in the community may very well want done. But they are not legal.

9-1c Cops As Administrative Actors

The police are legal, political, and administrative actors, all rolled into one. In the administrative arena, the police must live by the rules of conduct set down by police professionals in police department "general order manuals." This third set of standards makes up the "nuts and bolts" of police work. These standards are the focus of much of the training the police experience.

Neither the courts nor the people have much to say, for example, about how to fill out appropriate forms, how to handcuff a suspect, how to search a prisoner, how to transport an arrestee, and so forth. All of the general orders or specific "how to be a cop" regulations that cover such behavior are written by police managers. Along with them, in general order manuals, are many other rules relating to job performance. These include regulations about tardiness, sick leave time off, grooming, proper uniform display, and so on. The police must abide by these rules and will be punished if they ignore them.

Thus, police officers must answer to three separate sets of standards. They must observe the law, respond to the community, and follow profession regulations. Of course, being human beings and operating under great stress at all hours of the day and night, they will sometimes violate the norms of conduct that are included in these standards. But in failing to live up to different sets of standards and in being influenced by different types of motivations, erring police officers will be guilty of different kinds of misconduct.

9-2 Different Types of Misconduct

Police misconduct falls into five distinctive category types. To illustrate the differences in these types, we begin by discussing two sets of parameters that define them. Two questions must be asked of police misconduct for us to fit such misbehavior into its proper place in a typology. First, was the misbehavior done in the name of personal gain? That is, did the police officer(s) involved seek to profit personally from the misconduct? Whether it takes the form of money, goods, services, or other types of trade-offs, when police officers misbehave they are either looking to enhance their own material well being or they are not.

Second, did the misconduct involve the use of the police officer's legal authority? That is, did the cop "sell the badge" in exchange for something? Whether it involves protecting criminals from arrest or arresting certain criminals to enhance the business of others, police officers sometimes use their legal state-granted authority as a bargaining tool to get something accomplished that is improper. On the other hand, sometimes their legal authority has nothing to do with police misconduct.

Once these two questions are answered, police misconduct can be classified into its five major types. Four fall into a table, and one exists outside of that table. This may seem to be just an academic exercise, but it is not. The consequences, methods of investigation, punishments, and political fallout associated with each of these five types of misbehavior are

TABLE **9-1** Typology of Police Misconduct

		For Personal Gain?	
		Yes	No
Misusing Legal Authority?	Yes	Corruption of authority	Noble cause corruption
	No	Police crime	Ineptitude

different—sometimes very different—from each other. Furthermore, our ethic to live by can have very different things to say about the relative immorality of the various types.

Table 9-1 shows how four of the types of police misconduct are determined by applying our two questions above. Let us discuss these types individually.

9-2a Corruption of Authority

Police officers are guilty of what we label "corruption of authority" when they misuse their legal authority (badges) to obtain personal rewards. This takes several forms. Payoffs are sometimes obtained by police officers to protect certain criminal enterprises, such as gambling, prostitution, and drug sales. Money is handed over to the police, and arrests are not made. Shakedowns are sometimes undertaken wherein police officers proactively demand money from people, normally small business operators, in exchange for "letting them off easy" with regard to city ordinances and so forth. Graft is sometimes accepted on an individual basis, from a motorist in exchange for not giving a ticket for example, or for not administering the law in an impartial manner.

> *"Well, I'm all broken up about his [the criminal's] "rights."*
> *What about her [the victim's] rights?"*
> — Clint Eastwood in *Dirty Harry*

9-2b Noble Cause Corruption

A few years ago, the "Dirty Harry Problem" was labeled by noted criminologist Carl Klockars (see "The Dirty Harry Problem" in *Moral Issues in*

Policing, Elliston and Feldberg, eds., Totowa, N.J., 1985). He stated that some police officers ignore the due process limitations of the law during investigations and/or in handling nonlegal details. They do this to get the job done. That is, to deter criminals and/or to prosecute people they believe are guilty of criminal deeds, cops will write false reports, harass citizens, and use excessive force. (When noble cause corruption involves lying on the witness stand to obtain a conviction, it is called "testilying.") All of these sorts of behaviors involve police officers misusing their legal authority and improper ways, but they are not doing so for personal gain. "Getting the bad guys behind bars"—not making money—is the rationalization here. Thus, it is considered a noble-cause type of corruption.

9-2c Police Crime

Sometimes, police officers will become involved in criminal activities while on duty that do not involve the use of their legal offices. Cops will sometimes use the opportunities that being on duty, particularly at night, afford to them to burglarize businesses or residences. Sometimes, when a theft has already occurred, police officers will take merchandise or money and report it as part of the original theft. When this type of misconduct happens, cops are misbehaving to obtain personal gain. But they are not trading off their legal authority to do so. Thus, this type of misconduct is considered different from either of the above two types.

9-2d Ineptitude

There are all sorts of transgressions against departmental regulations that are considered to be police misconduct but that involve neither personal gain nor the misuse of police legal authority on the part of erring cops. Such common violations as sleeping on duty, showing up habitually late, writing poor reports, failing to respond to calls, and ignoring orders make up this category. While these are serious violations when investigated, they are neither criminal nor corrupt in their nature. They are thus considered to be merely the products of ineptitude.

9-2e Personal Misbehavior

In this category belong sorts of personal (and sometimes even criminal) misconduct that reflect on an officer's image as a police officer but that have nothing to do with actual police officer performance on duty. Here we are talking about alcoholism, cohabitation, off-duty drunk driving, and so on. This category does not fit on our chart of types of misconduct because it does not directly relate to a person acting as a police officer.

However, we should not make the mistake of thinking that police officer behavior off duty is unimportant. It has great significance in two ways. First, police officer misconduct during the off-duty hours of one's personal life may be of general relevance to the image of a police department. When a police officer cheats on his or her taxes, for example, it can have a tremendous, negative effect on community confidence in the police. Thus, an officer found guilty of "conduct unbecoming an officer" can be disciplined even if the conduct has no relation to anything he or she ever did on duty. This is because the perceptions of the public toward the police are critical to maintaining legitimacy in any police organization.

Second, the way in which a police officer behaves off duty is directly controlled by the kind of person that police officer is. That is, it relates to his or her character. Because of this, off-duty behavior is just as critical as on-duty behavior as an indicator of police ethics. One does not become a different person when one goes to work. Certainly we are all familiar with the idea that people change roles when they enter their job environments. But they do not change the basic nature of who they are, how they think, and how they moralize. This element of character is constant. Thus, this category is critical to our discussion. See box 9-3.

9-3 Police Review Systems

While this book cannot delve deeply into police review systems and their operations, we will take just a moment here to consider why this scheme to differentiate types of misconduct is important. Police officers can be the subjects of either criminal investigations or administrative investigations. When they are subject to criminal investigations, police officers are targeted either by internal affairs, by departmental detectives (burglary detectives or rape detectives, for example), or by local prosecutors and their investigative staffs. Where departments are large enough, such investigations are usually kept "in house." For smaller departments, it is customary to pass such investigations on to the local prosecutor. This is done to avoid the appearance of a conflict of interest on the part of investigators who are themselves police officers.

When cops are accused of either noble cause corruption or ineptitude, they are almost always investigated by internal affairs. It is completely appropriate for this to be the case. No external police agency is

Box 9-3

Presidential Misconduct

Recent political scandals involving various U.S. presidents help to illustrate the different types of misconduct we are discussing. It is interesting to remember these events and to reflect on how we tend to consider some of them "heinous" and some of them "forgivable" depending on our personal political views.

Corruption of Authority = In his last week as president, George Bush issued a pardon to everyone involved in the Iran/Contra scandal. In doing so, he excused several people from prosecution, one of whom was about to argue in court that he was ordered to commit crimes by both Presidents Reagan and Bush. Thus, Bush's blanket pardon saved his own skin. This is Corruption of Authority because Bush used his power as president for his own personal gain.

Noble Cause Corruption = When President Ronald Reagan allowed Oliver North to organize the delivery of arms to the Contras in Nicaragua, using drug dealers to accomplish this criminal task, Reagan was guilty of Noble Cause Corruption. What Reagan did was illegal, but he did not personally profit from it. On the contrary, Reagan was convinced that these crimes were perpetrated "in the best interests" of America.

Criminal Behavior = When the Watergate scandal broke, it implicated President Richard Nixon in dozens of crimes and almost all of our types of misconduct. One thing the president did was steal leftover campaign funds to buy expensive gifts for his wife. This is criminal behavior that did not relate to his official capacity as president. His office simply presented to him the opportunity to commit this crime.

Ineptitude = When President Jimmy Carter ran for re-election in 1980, voters held him accountable for what millions considered ineptitude—his inability to solve the Iranian hostage crisis and to return home more than 100 Americans being held hostage by the Iranians. This was a classic example, as determined by voters, of ineptitude that had to be rectified via the ballot box.

Personal Misbehavior = When he was impeached and tried in the Senate, President Bill Clinton was accused of personal misconduct. The reason he was acquitted, and the reason his popularity soared during this time frame, was a majority of Americans believed his conduct to be improper but not a reflection of the job he was doing as president. His extramarital affair was thus considered personal misconduct by a large number of people.

required for this purpose. Such investigations are not criminal in nature; they are administrative. They are either initiated by internal sources (for example, supervisors who report habitual tardiness) or by citizens' complaints of a noncriminal nature. The same can be said for personal misbehavior problems. Such investigations can be handled by supervisors or by internal affairs.

Two points now present themselves. The first involves corruption of authority. While internal, police departmental organizations (internal affairs) can attempt to uncover and investigate corruption of authority, this is not always possible. Corruption of authority by the police can often involve long-term, organized systems of extortion and bribery that so completely permeate the subcultural structure of a police organization that they cannot be effectively controlled by members of that same organization. Such misconduct must be investigated by authorities outside the police departmental system in which it occurs. The reasons for this will become clear when we delve more deeply into the nature of corruption of authority in chapter 10.

The second point is civilian review. Civilian review boards have been instituted in about 50 jurisdictions throughout the United States in recent years. The idea of civilian review, of course, is to bring an outside, non-police perspective to the problem of investigating police misconduct. Especially with regard to citizens' complaints, civilian review is a concept based on the logic that the police cannot be trusted to police themselves. Feeling that the "blue code of silence" will make police officers prone to protect their fellow officers and not take police accountability seriously, civilian review attempts to generate higher standards of thoroughness and objectivity than those that are presumably present in internal affairs organizations.

Civilian review is hotly debated wherever it is attempted. Police officers almost universally think it will be unfair to the police and will take the citizens' side when complaints are investigated. Civilians, on the other hand, believe that police-operated internal affairs systems will take the police officers' side and will not be honest and fair in weighing the citizens' side of a complaint.

Study in civilian review has found that neither argument is correct. On one hand, civilian review finds the police guilty of misconduct less often than does internal review. Thus, it does not treat police officers unfairly. On the other hand, civilian review does not side with citizens

Box 9-4

Some Facts About Civilian Review Boards

- They do not find the police guilty more often than do internal affairs.
- They are not abusive of individual police officer rights.
- They are extremely expensive to run.
- They create more community faith in the idea that the police are accountable.

(See Douglas W. Perez, *Common Sense About Police Review*, Temple University Press, 1994.)

often, and thus might be considered in some sense a waste of time. It spends a lot of money and does not come to conclusions that are different than those reached by internal systems. Thus, civilian review may be an important tool in generating the perception that the police are being held accountable for their actions, but it "satisfies" no one—not the police and not citizen complainants—in a substantially different way than does internal review. See box 9-4.

This debate is complicated and confusing. It is enough to say that civilian review can be an alternative to internal systems for the purposes of investigating citizens' complaints of police misconduct when the perceived legitimacy of police-operated systems is called into question. Furthermore, it is safe to say that civilian review boards do not have the expertise and investigative power to curb corruption of authority or criminal behavior on the part of the police. Thus, civilian review can have a limited yet potentially positive impact on police misbehavior. It can generate a feeling in a community that the police are being held to community-based standards of behavior and are not protected by some sort of police subcultural prejudice.

Summary

In chapter 9, we have discussed the three types of standards to which the police must be held accountable. We also unveiled a typology that identified several different kinds of misconduct into which police officers sometimes fall. It is important to define clearly what those forms take before proceeding with an appraisal of how our ethic to live by should be applied to police work by the modern, professional police officer. It is toward a consideration of how that should be done that we now turn.

Topics for Discussion

1. There is no one cause of crime. Similarly, there is no one cause of police misconduct. Discuss some of the multiple causes of criminal deviance and make analogies to the multiple causes of police deviance.
2. Discuss how cleaving to the law and listening to the interests of their constituents—the citizens—can create confusion for the police. What are some examples of circumstances under which police officers are asked by law-abiding citizens to do things that are illegal and professionally unethical?
3. Chapter 9 explored five types of misconduct: corruption of authority, noble cause corruption, criminal behavior, ineptitude, and personal misbehavior. Think of examples of each. Compare and contrast them.

1920

WW1 - (1914-1918)

Raaring 20's = prosparity

-Prohibition- No alchohol, it is illegal- it led to
Moral decay.
a. There is a demand for alcohol so there
has to be a supply.

Joseph Kennedy was the #1 bootleger &
part of organized crime (OC).

- finances on the rise

Cracks in banking system

women were giving a right to vote.

-Great Depression (1928-29)

1964, 43 years ago the Civil Rights Act
was passed.

1930's (1932 Berlin Olympics)(Jesse Owens sprinter

-Stock market Crash

- In Russia Communist took over & that led to
food lines, unemployment and people loosing
everything they own.
- Germany; The Hitler party believed in Nationalism
Socialism.

Franklin D. Rosevelt; he was a democratic,
he created SSN, Medicaid, medicare, WPA &
the, public Assisted living.
- WWII - late 30's - Unions

late 40's we were finghting a nonsense war

1950's - prosparity - DDE - Republican

Joseph McCarthy senator of Wisconsin who went afte
Hollywood & the military. while fighting Russia & Sov
union were our enemies.

law enforcement: FBI was taking a more active role in
organized crime of the 5 families.

[Handwritten at top of page:] Communism · Everybody produces for the good of a whole. Socialism— Government handles everything

Corruption of Authority and Police Crime

10

> "Police corruption has existed for as long as police themselves have existed. Nearly all urban police departments in the United States have been touched by corruption scandals at some time in their history."
> — Stephen Light, Sociologist

Outline

In chapter 10, we group together two types of misconduct from our typology in chapter 9, namely corruption of authority and police crime, because they both involve the abuse of the police officer's duty in a similar way. Both include the dynamic of officers misbehaving to obtain personal gain. Because this is so, we ought to be able to argue to any police officer, would-be police officer, student of criminal justice, or even interested citizen that such behavior is absolutely unacceptable.

There is no way to apply utilitarian ethics to misconduct that involves personal gain in an effort to rationalize it. Thus, when we view corruption of authority and/or police crime, we are prone to take a somewhat Kantian, absolutist viewpoint. No amount of special circumstances or rationalization can make these types of conduct appear to be ethical. As Kant might say, using a position of trust to obtain personal gain is wrong, not just some of the time but all of the time and in all circumstances.

Applying our ethic to live by, we conclude that corruption of authority and police crime involve violations of the primary duty of the police, the first rule by which they must abide in cleaving to the principle of beneficence—namely, to do no harm. When the police avoid this duty and act for personal gain, the community suffers and respect for the law is impaired.

But there is a problem with taking this absolute position. First, it ignores how and why such misconduct is sometimes generated among police officers—it tends to allow us to avoid studying its causes. Second, it ignores how these types of behaviors are rationalized after the fact. While it might seem to many that no amount of excuse making could make anyone accept this type of behavior as legitimate, this simply isn't so. Some police officers do, in fact, believe corruption of authority and/or police crime are "understandable" behaviors.

And because they are sometimes rationalized, corruption of authority and, to a lesser extent, police crime, have always been problems associated with the police. (See box 10-1.) While these two types of misconduct have lessened to a great extent in recent years, they are still with us. They constitute significant problems for police administrators, for honest police officers, and for the public in general.

In approaching this unfortunate reality, chapter 10 will first analyze some of the causes of these types of misconduct and then discuss some of the rationalizations some police officers, and in some places the entire police subculture, create to make them seem acceptable. Then, we will apply our ethic to live by to these misconduct types. To begin with, we will discuss the roots of corruption of authority and police crime.

10-1 Causes

Crime is often the product of the greed of individuals combined with opportunities presented by life's circumstances. While we could take time

Box 10-1

Review of Definitions

Corruption of authority = Police officers obtaining personal gain by misusing their legal authority ("selling their badges")

Police crime = Police officers obtaining personal gain without misusing their authority

here to discuss a number of theories about the causes of crime, we will stick to a consideration of greed and opportunity because they are central to the problems of police corruption of authority and police crime.

People possess a natural tendency to want to enhance their personal financial situations and that of their families. This propensity is in all of us, and it is not necessarily a bad thing. It is the dynamic that drives capitalism. The capitalistic system expects everyone to behave in a (somewhat) greedy fashion. In a capitalistic economy, all citizens attempt to further their own financial situations by competing in the open marketplace. To do this, they attempt to work harder, produce more goods, provide better services, create more significant innovations, and invent better products than their competitors. When they are successful, people make more money and have (arguably) better lives than those whom they "defeat" in this competition.

Thus, when channeled in this positive way, greed works to make life better for individuals, for their families, and for the general public. In the larger scheme of things, this type of capitalistic greed produces a better life for almost everyone. It provides the motivation that drives the American economic engine that has been the envy of the world for generations.

In police officers, too, greed can be a good, positive force. To further their own positions in life, for example, police officers may be moved to seek assignments that are difficult and dangerous, to obtain positions that involve increased responsibilities, to get promoted, and generally to do good works and a competent job to obtain increased status and/or income. Not only is there nothing wrong with this, but it also presents to us the best example of how the capitalistic, competitive spirit can be applied to police work. Our ethic to live by might suggest that doing good, with personal greed as the rationale, is still doing good.

But when people's individual greed moves them to break the rules, to circumvent the law, and to take unfair advantage of others, it becomes a form of deviance. In the police officer, this type of deviance is particularly troublesome because it involves the abuse of the position of trust into which the criminal justice system has placed the cop on the beat. The duty of police officers is, quite clearly, to perform their many tasks and multiple roles in the interests of justice and with an eye to providing services and protection to all of society's members. When this duty is convoluted and ignored in favor of personal gain, the interests of justice are at risk.

So greed can be bad or good, depending on the character of the individual. In people who are prone to want more no matter what it takes, and who are thus prone to cheat, lie, and take shortcuts, greed is bad. It moves them to ignore their duties as police officers, citizens, fathers, mothers, and so on in favor of furthering their own situations, financial, political, or other.

When people who possess this type of character flaw are confronted with the opportunity to obtain personal gain at the expense of others, they may be prone to commit all sorts of criminal acts. Such people may cheat on their taxes, calculating that the IRS will probably not investigate their phantom deductions. They may pad a theft insurance claim, calculating that there is no way for anyone to know what specifically was stolen. Or they may take the opportunity at work to skim some money from the till, knowing that no one else is watching.

Police officers are often presented with such opportunities. The police occupy a position of trust. More often than most people, police officers are in a position to abuse that trust if they possess the type of character that moves them to do so. With regard to the corruption of authority, the police often interact with criminals—especially those involved in victimless crimes such as drug trafficking, gambling, and prostitution—who will offer to reimburse the police if they "look the other way." There is so much profit involved in such types of crimes that the pressure to sell the badge by not making arrests in exchange for money is great.

But the police also have opportunities presented to them that do not involve selling their positions or misusing their legal authority for personal gain. At night, operating largely alone, police officers will learn which businesses are vulnerable to theft, which doors are left open, which establishments have a lot of cash on hand, and so on. When thefts occur, for example, police officers are often presented with the opportunity to skim some money or goods before anyone else arrives at a crime scene. This, as opposed to the corruption of authority, is police crime.

The opportunities presented to the police are so great as to (almost) guarantee that some police officers will take advantage of them. Those who possess a certain limited understanding of their roles, the importance of police ethics, and the nature of professionalism will exhibit their personal character flaws in this way. They will become involved in corruption of authority and/or in police crime.

Thus, greed—which is present in all people and all police officers—will meet with opportunity—which is presented to police officers in a way that it is not often presented to civilians—to produce the tendency toward these types of misconduct. Given how much of police work is done alone and unobserved, personal character (as we have argued all along) is the one and only hedge the police officer can possess that mitigates falling into such misconduct.

10-2 Grass Eating, Meat Eating, and the Slippery Slope

Those who study police corruption of authority and police crime have developed a labeling scheme to illustrate different levels of misconduct. They refer to "grass eating" and "meat eating." We will discuss this differentiation and discuss how it helps us to understand the generation of these types of misconduct.

10-2a Grass Eating

Grass eating involves two types of police behavior (or misbehavior). First, it entails a nonsystematic, individualized type of personal gain-related misconduct that sometimes develops from individual police–citizen interactions. This type of misconduct is not proactive in the sense that the police who become involved in it do not seek out citizens as victims and do not attempt to glean large amounts of graft. Thus, grass eating includes accepting cash in exchange for not writing a moving violation, obtaining police discounts, eating free food, drinking free coffee, and so on. While these activities are all unacceptable because they do harm to the image of the police and the law, they nevertheless are considered by students of police misconduct to be "minor" in their importance.

Second, grass eating involves the acceptance by some police officers of the large-scale, organized (meat-eating) misconduct of others. That is, grass eating also involves looking the other way and not reporting/taking action with regard to the personal gain-related misconduct of others. Thus, some police officers who never take payoffs of any kind can still be considered to be grass eaters if they become of aware of meat eating and take no action to stop it. This type of behavior involves another transgression against our ethic. It ignores the duty to remove evil.

10-2b Meat Eating

Meat eating involves proactive, systematic, organized payoffs. Examples include narcotics officers who accept money on a regular basis in exchange for not arresting certain drug dealers, vice officers who accept money from pimps in exchange for not arresting their prostitutes, and beat cops who regularly shake down businesses and demand protection money from them. When officers actively seek opportunities to obtain personal gain and organize systems for accepting and covering up such behavior, they are meat eating. (Again, when anyone else in the police world sees this happening and looks the other way, they are grass eating.)

10-2c The Slippery Slope

Numerous authors in several different fields of deviance study have discussed the idea of the "slippery slope" (see box 10-2). This idea suggests that when people begin to deviate, they do so in small, incremental ways. But once a person strays from norms and rules of conduct, he or she begins to slide down a slope that leads to greater, more pronounced forms of deviance. Thus, kids begin with shoplifting and then "graduate" to burglary and perhaps even armed robbery. Business people begin with phantom tax deductions and eventually bury large amounts of income in elaborate tax evasion schemes. And so it goes.

With regard to police officer misconduct, the slippery slope idea suggests that grass eating supports meat eating in two ways. First, some officers who first accept small gifts such as free coffee or free meals eventually will begin to normalize accepting more significant gifts such as money from drug dealers or pimps in exchange for allowing these people to violate the law. Especially in departments with a history of organized corruption schemes—and these departments still exist—where misconduct is rampant, the slippery slope idea suggests grass eating is the precursor to organized, systematic corruption. Thus, grass eating develops into meat eating.

A second way grass eating relates to meat eating is that, as discussed above, grass eating also can involve looking the other way when meat eat-

Box 10-2

Can "a Little Bit of Graft" Be a Good Thing?

In an era when community-based policing requires police officers to create permanent bonds with their communities, a number of strategies are being used to accomplish this task. One such tactic, suggested by authors such as Robert Kania, is for individual police officers to move closer to the people on their beats by accepting graft of the "minor" sort, such as free cups of coffee, free meals, or police discounts. The idea is that people and police officers will bond and feel closer to each other through this sort of personalized interaction.

Those who believe in the slippery slope idea of police misconduct are strongly opposed to this argument. They see the acceptance of such "minor" gratuities as grass eating, which will almost invariably lead to meat eating. Thus, some believe Kania's idea is a genuinely dangerous one for today's police officers. For them, there is no such thing as "minor" amounts of unethical behavior. They, being believers in ethical formalism, reject the utilitarian idea that some graft can be good.

There is another school of thought that cuts through the middle of this argument. Aristotle would say that such community-building, minor gratuities are acceptable if the officer(s) involved possess the good character not to consider such gifts as bribes. In other words, as long as officers treat those who give them free coffee appropriately, fairly, and without preference when they become involved with the police in legal situations, accepting such gifts is ethical and appropriate.

(Note: For a discussion of this debate about "acceptable levels of graft," see Joycelyn Pollock's *Ethics in Crime and Justice*.)

ing occurs. When officers are discovered to be involved in organized, systematized payoffs, grass eating officers ignore it. For large-scale, organized payoffs to continue indefinitely, there usually must be a tacit acceptance of this behavior by officers who are not directly involved. Thus, even if grass eating does not create meat eating, it perpetuates it; grass eating by the many is necessary for meat eating by the few.

Thus, the slippery slope idea suggests small-scale graft is unacceptable because it cannot be differentiated from large-scale graft. While there certainly is a quantitative difference between a free cup of coffee and taking large amounts of money from drug dealers, the slippery slope idea posits that there is no qualitative difference.

10-3 Rationalizations

While this is not a text that can delve deeply into the causes of police deviance, we want briefly to engage subcultural and individual dynamics that tend to help errant police officers rationalize their deviant ways.

10-3a Subcultural Rationalizations

Those who study what is referred to as the police subculture often speak as if there is only one type of subculture associated with police work. However, this simplistic idea is not realistic. There are as many different types of police subcultures as there are different types of police departments. And the differences in the dynamics that operate within these subcultures are particularly pronounced when related to police misconduct.

In some jurisdictions, the police subculture is a loosely knit group of men and women who merely happen to be co-workers in the same occupation. In such places, officers share a perspective about life on the beat, about their roles and duties, and about police professionalism and competence. In such jurisdictions, police misconduct is seen as a problem for every officer because it impacts the respect citizens hold for the police. Furthermore, when police misconduct of the personal gain type is investigated in such organizations, cooperation is obtained from the overwhelming majority of police officers.

In other jurisdictions—happily a steadily decreasing number of police organizations—personal gain-oriented misconduct is normalized and at least tacitly accepted throughout the (very tightly knit) subculture. Fighting such misconduct, therefore, becomes extremely difficult because attempts to hold errant officers accountable are opposed, even by those who do not participate in personal gain-type misconduct. Cleaving to what many authors call the "blue code of silence" even would-be honest officers who know about corruption of authority and/or police crime often do not cooperate in its investigation. Such reluctance by grass eaters to help with the pursuit of systematic misconduct can effectively guarantee meat eaters will cover up their misconduct and pursue it on a continuous basis.

10-3b Individual Rationalizations

In some places, the entire police subculture supports a personal gain-type of misconduct. More often, however, rationalizations for police misconduct are very similar to rationalizations criminals use to neutralize their

T A B L E **10-1** Police Techniques of Neutralizing Deviance

Neutralization Technique	Verbalization	Police Context
1. Denial of Responsibility	"They made me do it."	Citizens offer graft and the police officer takes it to be the "norm."
2. Denial of Injury	"No 'innocents' got hurt."	Police take money from drug dealers and not "honest citizens."
3. Denial of Victim	"They deserved it."	Police thefts occur "because" business owners are not careful.
4. Condemning the Condemners	"They don't know anything."	Police rejection of legal and department control and sanction of deviant behavior.
5. Appeal to Higher Loyalty	"Protect your own."	Police perjury to protect another officer.

Source: Victor E. Kappeler, Richard D. Sluder, and Geoffrey P. Alpert. *Forces of Deviance*, 2nd Ed., Waveland Press, 1998; op. cit., 114.

deviant acts. That is, individual officers, or small groups of them, neutralize feelings of guilt over deviant behavior using five distinctive techniques.

Studying deviance in 1957, authors Gary Sykes and David Matza suggested there are several ways people can rationalize their misbehavior and avoid the normally negative self-image that goes with it. Since that time, several authors (including Kappeler et al. in table 10-1) have applied this idea to misbehaving police officers. We will briefly review these techniques here.

First, police officers can deny they are responsible for their own actions. They can view their acts as predetermined by people, events, and situations they cannot influence. Thus, well meaning citizens, liberal judges, the thoughtless press, "spoiled brat" intellectuals, the due process system, and a host of other people and institutions are responsible for somehow requiring the police to misbehave. An example might be the officer who takes police discounts because "the store owner would be offended if I didn't."

Using a second technique for neutralizing deviance, police officers can deny their misbehavior caused any injury. Much like citizens who rationalize cheating on their income taxes or defrauding wealthy insurance companies, police officers can tell themselves no one was really hurt by their deviance. An example might be officers who take merchandise from a burglary site rationalizing "no one gets hurt" by it.

The third technique of neutralization involves the denial of the victim. Because of the character of the victim of police misconduct, it is possible to deny there was any misconduct. If the people "ripped off" are drug dealers, violent gang members, or criminals of some other type, they do not have the right to status as victims.

Fourth, errant police officers may condemn the condemners. Here, police officers may accuse those who accuse them of misconduct. Lawyers from civil liberties groups, the investigators in internal affairs, or judges who scrupulously attack corrupt police officers are all at fault. This technique shifts responsibility away from the misbehaving officers toward others.

Finally, the deviant police officer may appeal to higher loyalties. By protecting other deviant officers, by going along with corruption schemes, or by interfering with investigations into police misconduct, police officers may feel they are supporting their fellow officers and the subculture in general. In doing so, they invoke a loyalty and a duty that circumvent their duty to the law and to the community.

In these ways, erring police officers rationalize their misbehavior and avoid dealing with what we have called the duty to be beneficent. They do harm to others (in the form of meat eating or committing police crime) or they fail to remove harm (in the form of grass eating). Because it has been studied by many criminologist and psychologists, we might acknowledge that such rationalizing is understandable in some sense. But just as we are prone to deny criminals their rationalizations, we can and must acknowledge police crime and corruption of authority exhibit character flaws that cannot be tolerated in the competent, professional officer.

10-4 Fighting Corruption of Authority and Police Crime

We will find in chapters 11 and 12 that attempting to deter some types of police misconduct, especially noble cause corruption, is extremely difficult because police officers defend it so vehemently. This is not usually the case with the two forms discussed in chapter 10. Thus, we will have a very brief and straightforward discussion here about what to do about such behavior.

Corruption of authority and police crime can be approached proactively through intelligently managed police selection, training, and education systems. Choosing the right kind of people to be police officers—those with the character the job requires—and then giving them appropriate training can have a lasting effect on such behavior. Police administrators at both the supervisory and the management levels can lead the way. Personal character, as always, is key. Officers who do not see themselves as professionals, who do not take beneficence seriously, will be prone to fall into such behavior. Those who take our arguments, and themselves, seriously will have little trouble avoiding becoming rouge police officers.

In dealing with corruption of authority and police crime retroactively, there are two different solutions. Grass eating can be dealt with using internal investigatory methods (internal affairs) or even civilian review. Because of its limited nature, this type of problem tends to be idiosyncratic and can be dealt with as such. The officer who is concerned about his or her own professionalism and who takes police professionalism seriously can and must participate in the application of this solution. In other words, he or she must cooperate with investigators. Beneficence requires this.

In dealing with meat eating, however, police organizations must face the inevitable fact that such behavior is not limited to isolated, "bad apple" cops. In such situations, external review by outside police agencies or by federal officials is necessary. When police misconduct of these types is widespread, accepted, and covered up, the only way progress can be made is through the agencies of honest professionals from outside the organization. Again, the individual officer concerned about professionalism, while having an admittedly limited impact, can and must cooperate with such investigations in the name of creating professionalism and in the name of beneficence.

10-5 What Can One Officer Do?

In police organizations where personal gain-type misconduct is not the normal order of things, it is easy enough to avoid it. The personal commitment an individual of good character makes to avoid such behavior is sustained in such organizations by a subculture-wide understanding that any and all misbehavior must be avoided if all police officers are to enjoy the fruits of genuine professionalism.

Box 10-3

The Story of Frank Serpico

Frank Serpico was a young man in New York who had always wanted to be a police officer. His dramatic story has been told in several books and in a popular Hollywood movie. Serpico was sworn in as a New York police officer in the 1960s. Surrounded by corruption, both on the part of uniformed officers and detectives, Serpico vowed never to take graft and to do his job honestly. To begin with, he was left alone by corrupt officers and seen as a sort of comic figure in the department.

But when he worked his way up the assignment ladder and became a detective, this changed. Serpico began to receive threats relating to the corruption he was avoiding. The corruption he witnessed was so rampant and offended his sense of ethics so profoundly that he began to participate in internal investigations into corruption. This participation amplified the threats to the extent that he feared for his life. He feared corrupt police officers would kill him to cover up their misdeeds.

Eventually he was shot on duty, attempting a drug bust, under circumstances that suggested he was left without cover by his fellow (corrupt) cops. Frank Serpico had to retire at a very young age from his beloved profession because of the bullet that remained lodged in his head and because both he and the department understood that his safety could never effectively be guaranteed.

In organizations that have a history of such misbehavior and that still maintain the blue code of silence, the road of the individual officer who wishes to avoid it may be much, much harder to travel. As the story of Officer Frank Serpico shows us (see box 10-3), it can be a long, lonely, uphill fight to avoid such temptations and to behave in a professional manner.

But that is no excuse for going along with behavior that is unethical. No good fathers or mothers would accept the "everybody's doing it" excuse from their children, and professional police officers cannot be any different. Finding those officers within the organization who are committed to genuine professionalism can help. Keeping in contact with them—professionals outside of such a deviant subculture—will avail the ethical officer of much-needed support.

In the long run, only the character of the individual can work toward professional competence and against such odds. We are left with the old adage, "It is better to light just one little candle than to curse the darkness."

Who you are and what you are made of is what avoiding these temptations is all about. The officer of good character will find within himself or herself the sustenance to do the job honestly, effectively, and ethically without reference to rationalizations and excuses about what others are doing.

Summary

This chapter has included two discussions about specific types of police misconduct: corruption or authority and police crime, which are linked together in a logical way. Both of these kinds of misbehavior involve police officers putting themselves and their own interests ahead of those of the law, the public, and (even) the police as a group. They both involve violations of our ethic to live by that are, in some sense, absolute in their impropriety.

We now turn from a discussion that was, in a real way, very straightforward, to one that is full of conceptual problems. In considering noble cause corruption and the Dirty Harry Problem, we will come face-to-face with police misconduct that is actually defended by a large number of those who perpetrate it. Thus, chapter 11 will present a completely different set of problems and a troublesome set of paradoxes for us.

Topics for Discussion

1. Consider the "slippery slope" idea. Discuss whether or not there is any difference between taking a police discount on tires at a local auto shop and taking money from drug dealers in exchange for not arresting them.

2. Discuss Kania's idea that "a little bit of graft can be good" for police–community relations. In an era of CBP, when the police are supposed to be forming tight bonds with the citizens on their beats, what do you think about Kania's assertion? Can "little graft" be kept separate from "big graft"?

3. Refer to table 10-1. Discuss the five ways people neutralize their feelings of guilt when they are deviant. Consider both police- and non-police-related examples.

Kefauver the senator of TN.

Civil Rights meant Social Unrest.

Media- people were seen on TV with police dogs biting them. (police brutality)

Integration- Harry S. Truman integrated the military.

1954- Brown vs. Board of Education

Seperate is never equal.

1960's- Sex

JFK was elected president and a democratic. young elected.

Peace workers were people who did good

Vietnam (1968)

Riots 1965-Watts Riot was the first one

Civil Rights Movements was at its peak

1968 Everything starts to fall apart

April 68 Martin is Killed

June 68 Bobby was killed.

Nixon was elected president and America lost its innocence.

1970-Knapp Commisson was founded.

Code of Silence means Omerta - Italian Organized Crime

levels of organization

Grass/Meat eaters-

Slippery Slope- if u start it will lead to Something else.

Reccomendations- Internal Affairs

2. Mangement/ Supervisors (LT/ Sgt runs the Dept.)

Education /training

Pay-Extra Jobs lead to corruption.

Noble Cause Corruption: Confronting Dirty Harry

> *"We're dealing with animals out there. They don't play by the rules. Why should we?"*
>
> — Veteran California officer to one of the authors, a rookie, in 1970

Outline

In chapter 10, we put together two types of misconduct and discussed them as one. That was a natural match because both corruption of authority and police crime involve the misconduct of police officers for personal gain. In chapter 11, we will focus on only one type of misconduct, noble cause corruption, and consider its causes, effects, and potential cures.

To review, noble cause corruption involves police officers misusing their positions of legal authority but not for personal gain. (See box 11-1.) Noble cause corruption presents a paradox for the student of police ethics because it involves behavior that appears to be unethical to those who view it from the outside but that is considered ethical by participants. This type of paradox is not present in our previous two types of misconduct. While some police officers will succumb to the temptation to become involved in the corruption of authority or in police crime, it is clear these types of behavior are unethical.

But the unethical nature of noble cause corruption is often not clear. Thus, we are faced with a sort of dilemma that is not presented by any other form of misconduct. Because of its very nature, noble cause corruption is accompanied by its own internal rationalization. Police officers who are involved in noble cause corruption are reluctant to acknowledge that it is unethical behavior because they believe it is necessary to get the job of policing done. They are involved, as the label states, in a noble cause, that of putting criminals behind bars and/or deterring criminal activity. Unlike those involved in police crime, for example, cops involved in noble cause corruption believe they are doing the right thing. This makes stopping such misconduct very difficult.

An additional problem with noble cause corruption is that the police can receive positive feedback from people in their communities when they engage in it. That is, citizens often want the police to get the job done at any cost. Police officers are told by people they see everyday to "get the gangs out of our neighborhood," "get the guns off of the streets," "keep drugs and drug dealers away from our kids," "lower the crime rate"—AND "we don't care how you do it." Thus, unlike any other form of misconduct, noble cause corruption is often accompanied by a significant amount of community support.

11-1 Definition: The Dirty Harry Problem

It has been almost twenty years since Carl Klockars wrote "The Dirty Harry Problem." In that article, he began to engage everyone in American police work with the idea that noble cause corruption was rampant and that it presented a tremendous problem for the rule of law. Klockars pointed out that police officers sometimes misbehave in an effort to do good work and to get their jobs done. That is, sometimes police officers

Box 11-1

The "Dirty Harry Problem"

Police officers are guilty of noble cause corruption when they misuse
their legal authority for reasons other than personal gain—when
they use their power, at least in their own eyes, to protect the community.
The "Dirty Harry Problem" is another label for noble cause corruption.

bend and/or break the due process rules of the American criminal justice
system to put people they believe to be factually guilty of criminal behavior behind bars. See box 11-2.

The due process system is made up of legal protections that the U.S.
Constitution affords to all criminal suspects. All people accused of committing crimes have the right to remain silent and not give evidence
against themselves. They have the right to obtain access to an attorney.
They have the right to a jury trial before their peers. They have a right to
confront witnesses against them, to be free from unreasonable searches
and seizures, to have a speedy trial, and so on. These protections make it
difficult to prosecute suspects successfully. They do not make it impossible, but they make it difficult.

From the perspective of those whose job it is to solve crimes, to find
out who did it, and to bring them to justice, these protections create roadblocks. These roadblocks inhibit prosecution in a way that seems artificial.
That is, when your job is to sift through evidence, interview witnesses, and
interrogate suspects, these rules of procedure seem to get in the way of
finding out the facts. They inhibit your ability to discover the substantive
truth about what happened when a crime was committed and about who
was responsible. When evidence such as physical evidence, statements
made by witnesses, or confessions made by suspects is excluded—thrown
out—by a court, it may seem to the police that the system has ignored the
facts. In this way, due process seems to fail to protect society from criminals and from crime in general.

This feeling, that the rules of the system get in the way, is a natural
one. Few who take seriously the job of protecting the innocent from the
guilty could think otherwise. But the competent, professional police officer of today must avoid the tendency to think the system is, therefore,
something to be ignored and (even) fought. There are very good reasons
for having the system's procedural rules in place, and the modern,

Box 11-2

"Dirty Harry" Callahan

In the 1970s, Clint Eastwood made the film character "Dirty Harry" famous in several Hollywood films, most notably the picture of the same name. Eastwood's character, San Francisco Homicide Detective Harry Callahan, was a tough, no-nonsense, "kick ass and take names" kind of police officer. Most important for our purposes, Dirty Harry never concerned himself with due process rules for interrogating suspects, collecting evidence, or conducting investigations. In fact, Harry thought the legal system was too complicated and that it was unfair to victims and police officers. So he had no respect for it.

The "Dirty Harry Problem" refers to the tendency of many in police work to rationalize their own illegal behavior due to the system's complicated, suspect's-rights-oriented nature. The Dirty Harry view of the system is used both to excuse police misconduct and to (essentially) "give up" on trying to do the job of policing in an ethical, legal, professional, competent manner.

---

educated, ethical officer must understand this. No amount of frustration on the part of police officers can be used to rationalize ignoring these rules and taking shortcuts to obtain prosecutions.

Dirty Harry presents students of police ethics with a particularly thorny problem because breaking the procedural laws of the due process system is done in the name of a noble cause: that of protecting society from the vicious, the cruel, the unprincipled who victimize the weak. This noble cause is one with which most members of the criminal justice system, most law-abiding citizens, and most police officers agree. The rationalization for noble cause corruption states, "So what if we broke the rules? We got the bad guy behind bars, and we protected society. We did the job we are paid to do."

In a troublesome way, noble cause corruption presents us with this dilemma: It appears that, in behaving like Dirty Harry, police officers cleave to the duty of beneficence. That is, in breaking the procedural rules of the criminal justice game, police officers are doing good. They are removing evil people from the streets. They are deterring criminals. And because of this view, noble cause corruption is by far the hardest form of police misconduct to deter.

Noble cause corruption takes several forms. First, it includes procedural, law-oriented types of misconduct. This involves falsifying evidence, making illegal searches, writing fictitious reports (sometimes referred to as "creative report writing"), lying to prosecutors, and committing perjury on the witness stand ("testilying."). All of these types of behavior are rationalized by some officers because they are seen as being necessary to ensure the police officer's job is done effectively. The police "break the law" (procedural law) to "enforce the law" (substantive law).

There is a second type of noble cause corruption that relates to creating a deterrent to crime. Police officers, being streetwise, common-sense-oriented people, know the deterrent impact of the criminal justice system's formal operations is limited. That is, people prone to criminal behavior are not often intimidated by laws on the books or by formal courtroom-oriented procedures when they (would-be criminals) calculate the chances of being caught and the likely penalties they might incur. Put bluntly, the law and formal legal procedures do not effectively intimidate the would-be criminal.

But the physical intimidation of would-be criminals by individual police officers and by the police in general does effectively intimidate them. Would-be deviants can be deterred from criminal acts if police officers advise them personally of the consequences of their behavior. If a cop tells a gang member face-to-face, "If I catch you with a gun again, I'll personally kick the crap out of you," the impact on the youth is likely to be far greater than everything else the entire criminal justice system threatens. Thus, the threat of having to answer to an individual police officer is far more intimidating, realistic, and threatening, than the possibility of being caught, arrested, charged, found guilty, and given a stiff sentence.

Furthermore, and this is a particularly troublesome reality, the use of excessive force in the name of the noble cause of deterrence is sometimes also rationalized. If suspects are regularly "roughed up" by the police, the word gets around that becoming a suspect will cost a person dearly. While some excessive force is the product of police ignorance or prejudice, a great deal of it is the product of the noble cause. Some officers see the limits of the rule of law, learn (on the other hand) the deterrent power of physical force, and resolve to use force—excessive, punishing force—to accomplish the job of deterring crime.

Therefore, police officers are faced with this dilemma: if they play by the rules of the game, they will be limited in their ability to deter crime. On the other hand, if they use their own powers of physical and psychological intimidation, directing them at those they believe might misbehave in a criminal manner, they can have tremendous success at deterring crime on the street. See box 11-3.

Box 11-3

The "Effectiveness" of Noble Cause Corruption

Several years ago, in a police jurisdiction on the West Coast, the officers who policed a high-crime area found they had a major problem with daylight burglaries on their beat. Through informants, they learned a significant amount of this burglary was being committed by a convicted burglar who had served hard time in the state penitentiary. This particular criminal was a very good burglar, in the sense that he was smart and could not be caught in the act. Thus, even though they knew he was a professional burglar and the victimizer of dozens of people on their beat, the police could not catch him.

The officers became even more frustrated when, on one occasion, the suspect was caught in the act and arrested, only to be turned loose because of a legal technicality. The arresting officers had conducted an illegal search of this suspect's car, and the evidence obtained was excluded (thrown out) in court.

Ignoring the suspect's constitutional rights, the officers began to stop him, on foot or when driving, every time they saw him. They conducted illegal searches of his car and ran records and warrants checks on a daily, sometimes hourly, basis. They generally harassed the man, taking up hours of his time and writing citations for the most questionable of infractions. He was finally given six months in the county jail for driving on a suspended license. When his six months were over and he was let out, he left the area never to be heard from again.

These officers, following their noble cause or answering to a higher duty than they considered the Constitution to present, had succeeded in removing a threat to the people of their community. Burglaries went down substantially, and the people on the beat were happy. Thus, noble cause corruption, in the form of harassment, had worked to do a job the criminal justice system could not accomplish legally.

It takes a firm commitment to the rule of law and a solid personal resolve to live by the dictates of the due process system for a police officer to avoid such behavior and do the job in a legally and ethically defensible way. In other words, avoiding the Dirty Harry Problem takes character. Furthermore, it involves cleaving to the second principle of our ethic to live by; it takes acknowledging that justice must be served and that it must be equally served to those we consider to be deviants.

11-2 The Ethical Implications of Dirty Harry-Like Behavior

What is wrong with using harassment, physical intimidation, excessive force, or "testilying" (to name only a few examples of noble cause corruption) if they get the job done? If it works to deter crime and to put away criminals—and if the deterrent impact of the criminal justice system doesn't work—then why not clean up the streets the way Dirty Harry did?

The answer is that breaking the rules involves breaking the law. And no amount of rationalizing can change police lawbreaking into something noble and just. It is what it is: police misconduct. And it is particularly unethical because it turns police officers into unprincipled enemies of the rule of law, precisely the types of people they profess to be fighting. Put another way, breaking procedural rules and thus becoming a lawbreaker involves the police officer in doing the harm (the promotion of evil).

It makes sense for us here to recall what the rule of law is. Human conduct can be acceptable and it can be unacceptable. It can be normal or it can be deviant. People can behave themselves or they can misbehave. The job of those who police is to deter misbehavior (prevent evil) and/or to deal with deviants by bringing them before authorities who are in the business of judging the extent of misbehavior and taking action accordingly (remove evil).

The key concept to remember is that what constitutes normal behavior and what constitutes deviance is, in a free and democratic society, determined by all of the people collectively. The people, through their elected representatives, make up the rules of behavior to which everyone must be held. The police do their best to apply those rules on the street. The courts, in turn, do their best to judge and to punish those who transgress against the rules. But the rules themselves are made by the citizens— the people—and not by the police.

Now, when the rules are broken, those responsible may or may not be caught. They may or may not be arrested by the police. Police discretionary decision-making power comes into play here. Often, when the police know who committed a crime—especially a minor one—they will not make an arrest. The police do, and should, exercise this power in the interests of justice.

But it is not the same on the other side of the law. That is, if a person has not committed a crime, then he or she cannot be arrested and, in fact, should not be subjected to any "curbside justice" type of punishment at

Box 11-4

The Framing of Rubin "Hurricane" Carter

Rubin "Hurricane" Carter, a world boxing champion in the 1960s, had had a troubled youth that included being arrested on several occasions. Despite a clean and honorable record of military service, he was hounded throughout his life by a New Jersey prosecutor who "knew" he was a bad person.

On one particular night when unknown suspects committed a murder in Carter's town, this prosecutor proceeded to manipulate witnesses and evidence in a way that put Carter behind bars for a crime that he did not commit. It took 20 years of Carter's life for him to be (finally) acquitted and given his freedom.

This was an example of the extent to which Dirty Harry-type thinking can create injustice. The local prosecutor, certain in his mind that Carter was a bad person and that he deserved to be behind bars, ruined this man's life in the name of doing good for the community.

---

the hands of the police. If people are not guilty of misbehaving, they should be left alone to pursue their own definitions of the good life. They are free to do this as long as they don't harm others.

Furthermore, the law must be administered equitably, without reference to race, color, national origin, sex, and so on (the second principle of our ethic). All of this is clear from our previous discussions. But the sticking point for those who become involved in noble cause corruption is the problem of proving guilt. The police may know or may think they know who is factually guilty of a crime. But until a person is proven to be guilty of misbehavior, the police can only investigate and apply the law objectively and fairly.

A distinction is often made between factual guilt and technical guilt. Sometimes we hear it made between substantive guilt and procedural guilt. The idea here, of course, is that owing to the operations of the due process system, some people who are factually (substantively) guilty are not found technically (procedurally) guilty. This is due to the practical, operational rules of the system. To use a personal "I know they're guilty" type of understanding as a substitute for legally proven guilt is to take the law into one's own hands. It involves ignoring the very essence of what law and rules are supposed to mean. See box 11-4.

Under the rationalization that they are involved in a noble cause, the police can interfere with this idealized view of the system. They can harass people they believe to be bad, even though they cannot catch them behaving badly. They can catch people behaving badly and, knowing the system will let them off, they can break the law to convict them. Or they can believe certain people are bad and completely invent legal cases against them by creating evidence, confessions, testimony, and so on.

In all of these cases, the police become a law unto themselves. When they do this, they break the law and thus become lawless. Noble cause corruption rationalizes this type of misconduct because those who are thus deterred and/or convicted are bad people and in some sense deserve it. But this attitude on the part of the police involves them (the police) being guilty of one of several things.

First, this type of noble cause corruption substitutes police intuition (which may or may not be correct) for legal, fair, equitable rules of procedure. When this happens, the police may be effective in deterring crime, but they may also become involved in creating crime. No matter how effective and correct the police are at knowing who is factually guilty, they are sometimes wrong. The implications of the police practice of "framing" suspects can be (1) that innocent people go to jail and/or (2) that anyone who witnesses this type of police behavior loses faith in the police, the system, and the law. In this way, the police both do harm and fail to distribute justice.

Second, this type of police misbehavior turns the police into criminals. Breaking the law is breaking the law. When people behave in a deviant manner, no matter what their personal rationalizations for it are, they are supposed to be held to answer for it. In a paradoxical way, those police officers who participate in noble cause corruption become part of the very same problem they are trying to solve. Because they look at due process as merely the rules of a complicated game, just as do the deviants they are framing, they become equally guilty of using the system to their personal advantage and avoiding the consequences of criminality. Again, they are doing harm.

"It is better to let one hundred guilty men go free than it is to convict an innocent man."
— **American Legal Axiom**

Third, and perhaps most important, when the police misbehave in this way, it takes away the entire rational base upon which the criminal justice system rests. In a free society we should be particularly concerned that no innocent people be punished. We take great pains to attempt to ensure this. Only the guilty are supposed to be punished, and they are suppose to be punished only when they deviate. When the agents of the system misbehave and are not punished—in fact, in the case of noble cause corruption, they insist their deviance is ethical—then the rationale for the system punishing anyone is lost.

Thus, noble cause corruption is the entire legal system's worst nightmare. It takes away the ability for us all to sleep easy at night knowing there are thousands of people in jail and prison. If the police are breaking the law with impunity and putting people in prison who may not be guilty, then we cannot or at least we should not rationalize holding anyone behind bars.

11-3 Noble Cause Corruption Strategies

What can be done about noble cause corruption if its central reason for existing is that so many people (and police officers) believe it is ethical to break the rules in pursuit of getting the job done? One strategy that combats noble cause corruption involves having police officers read, analyze, discuss, and debate it. Engaging in this sort of activity in advance of confronting the Dirty Harry Problem on the street is one way young police officers can prepare themselves to avoid its pitfalls.

Second, to avoid the Dirty Harry Problem, police officers must take their academic and skill-oriented studies seriously. If an officer is educated about search and seizure law, for example, then making up fictitious reports about how probable cause was obtained is not necessary. If an officer is expert in interrogation techniques, then giving Miranda warnings doesn't get in the way of obtaining information. If an officer knows the beat, has good contacts in the community, is trusted and respected (is a good community-based officer, in other words) then catching criminals in the act is easier. If officers are respected for their physical strength and defensive tactics and yet are known to be fair and impartial when dealing with people, then using excessive force to "put the fear of God into people" is not necessary. Competence, in other words, makes Dirty Harry-type behavior unnecessary. See box 11-5.

The critical point is that a well honed, common-sense-related understanding of life on the street, a sophisticated knowledge of the law, a

Box 11-5

Noble Cause Corruption—"The Big Excuse"

Underneath the ability to rationalize noble cause corruption lies the idea that the due process system is so complicated, so focused on legal technicalities, and so prone to protect criminals at the expense of victims that it cannot be an effective tool for fighting crime. Is this true?

In fact, it is not. We know this for any number of reasons. Two of them will be presented here. First, regarding one particular piece of procedural law—the requirement to advise suspects of their Miranda rights—a detailed study of the impact of Miranda was done by a police research group in Washington. The study found that after being admonished of their right to remain silent, 83% of all suspects made incriminating statements. This finding indicated that intelligent, educated, and professional police interrogators could live within the rules of Miranda and yet still obtain cooperation, information, and convictions from criminal suspects.

Second, six times as many convicts are incarcerated in America's state and federal prisons today than were there only twenty-five years ago. Even assuming some of these people have been "framed" by the processes of noble cause corruption, it is still obvious to even the most casual observer that the due process system does not make it "impossible" to convict guilty people.

Thus, for police officers to complain about the complications of the system is for them to become involved in making excuses about their inability to do the job—excuses that are simply not based in fact.

---

professional set of interrogation and investigation skills, and an intimate relationship with the community are all good hedges against needing the crutch of noble cause corruption to get the job done.

Thus, awareness of the noble cause corruption problem coupled with a sophisticated understanding of all of the skills the professional officer must posses can create a significant amount of insurance against the development of this type of misconduct. A consciousness of the ethical implications of Dirty Harry, born of the type of discussion presented in this book, adds to and enhances the other competencies mentioned above. They can all work together to mollify any tendency in professional officers to make excuses about the technicalities of the system, to ignore the rule of law, and to become a law unto themselves.

Summary

This discussion has confronted a type of police misconduct that is particularly troublesome given that it comes with its own, internally generated set of rationalizations. Police officers embarked upon the noble cause of getting the job done, arresting bad people (removing harm), and protecting society (doing good) can feel safe and secure within an understanding that they are behaving ethically.

The Dirty Harry Problem must be confronted. But the trouble is that police officers tend to be practical, no-nonsense, "real world" oriented individuals. The paradox of noble cause corruption is that while we may agree here in a theoretical discussion that is unethical, it can be seen to involve the practical application to crime problems on the street of techniques that do, in fact, "work."

In both chapters 10 and 11, we have engaged in discussions of types of police misconduct that are clearly troublesome for ethical officers and that are, in a real sense, the personal responsibilities of individual officers. In the next chapter, we will confront two distinctly different types of police misconduct. The first, ineptitude, is often inadvertent and not accompanied by any malicious intent whatsoever. Some ineptitude can be considered to be the responsibility of police leaders, and not of individual officers. The second, personal misconduct, is troublesome because it involves considering the personal, off-duty conduct of police officers and begs us to confront American values regarding individual (police officer) privacy.

Topics for Discussion

1. What is the "Dirty Harry Problem"? Discuss this idea of Klockars and come up with as many examples as you can of how police officers can fall into it.

2. Discuss the importance of factual guilt versus the importance of technical guilt. Focus on the necessity to protect innocent people from being found guilty and on the reality that the police are not always correct in their assumptions about people's guilt or innocence. Finally, think about how police officers feel and react when accused of misconduct and confronted by internal affairs. Do they not want a lawyer, want the chance to confront witnesses against them, and want the chance to make a thorough argument in their own defense?

3. Discuss box 11-5 and "the Big Excuse." While procedural safeguards do make it difficult to convict the guilty, doesn't the evidence in this box make you think that the job is still "doable" and that competent officers can get the job done in a legal and ethical way?

12

Ineptitude and Personal Misconduct

> *"Every time something goes wrong, they make a rule about it. All the directions in the force flow from someone's mistake. You can't go eight hours on the job without breaking the disciplinary code ... no one cares until something goes wrong. The job goes wild on trivialities."*
>
> — New York City Police Officer (quoted by Kappeler, et al., op. cit.)

Outline

Ineptitude and personal, off-duty misconduct are troublesome in different ways for different reasons. First, regarding ineptitude, when the police fail to do their jobs because of ineptness, their conduct often carries with it no intent to misbehave. Thus, a discussion of the causes and potential solutions for ineptitude does not engage us in considerations of culpability or blame that might be attached to conscious decisions to misbehave. Ineptitude often occurs almost inadvertently, usually without malice. Attempts to limit ineptitude, then, do not involve the sort of moralizing that all of our previous discussions have undertaken.

The second form of misconduct included in chapter 12, personal misconduct, presents another problem. In considering personal misconduct, we must enter into an analysis of what part of a police officer's private life, if any, is the business of the police department, the community, and the state. This presents a thorny issue because we live in a society that values personal freedom highly. As American citizens, police officers have rights to privacy like anyone else. Yet because they occupy roles as representatives of the state, police officers have some limits placed on their freedom of activity, even when off duty. Precisely what those limits are and should be is at issue in chapter 12.

We will begin with ineptitude. (See box 12-1.)

12-1 Police Ineptitude: Not Getting It Right

When police officers are guilty of ineptitude, they misbehave themselves, but they do so without obtaining personal gain and without abusing their legal authority. Ineptitude does not involve making decisions, conscious or unconscious, to engage in behavior that is unethical or appears to be unethical. Police officers who fail to do their duty because they are unintelligent, uneducated, not well trained, lazy, or unskilled have not chosen to misbehave in a way that would normally move an observer to label them as immoral.

But we must not go too far with the argument that ineptitude does not involve ethical decision making. We cannot make up excuses for inept officers. The responsibility for inept behavior still resides in the individual, ineffective officer. Being a competent police officer involves having the intelligence, education, motivation, and skill to get the job done and thus avoid ineptitude.

If an officer lacks any or all of these traits, he or she can (and should) be retrained, reeducation, or dismissed. An inept officer ought to be personally motivated to improve and also ought to be stimulated and encouraged by experienced leaders to change. Most techniques used for

Box 12-1

Review of Definitions

Ineptitude—Officers are guilty of ineptitude when they fail to get jobs done properly. This involves neither obtaining personal gain nor perverting their legal authority.

Personal Misconduct—Officers are guilty of personal misconduct when, off-duty and unrelated to their official capacities, they are guilty of deviance of some kind.

dealing with ineptitude involve proactive, "no-fault" strategies that bring change without impacting negatively upon an officer's career.

Ineptitude is often the product of inadvertent incompetence. When this is the case, police leaders can and should treat ineptitude in a positive, counseling-and-training mode. Thus, when officers write poor reports, they can be required to receive training in this area. When officers sleep on duty, motivation to cease this behavior can come from effective leadership. Many if not most inept officers, motivated by knowledgeable police leaders, can change their inept behavior in a way that it ceases to be a problem in the future. See box 12-2.

On the other hand, inept behavior is sometimes the product of problems that simply cannot be overcome. The lack of skills, knowledge, and perspective involved in some ineptitude is terminal in a sense. When officers are guilty of racism due to their personal beliefs about racial superiority, for example, they may have to be terminated. When officers are simply not intelligent enough to understand the nuances of the law, they may not be retrainable. And most importantly, when officers cannot or will not change themselves, when they do not respond to positive discipline in the forms suggested above, the system may eventually have to "give up" and dismiss the erring cops. Such problems involve character defects that sometimes simply cannot be corrected.

Thus, not all ineptitude is solvable and not all positive, motivational approaches to dealing with incompetence in a nonthreatening way will work. Police officer ineptitude is the product of several factors that can occur individually or in combination.

Some ineptitude is the result of poor selection processes. Some people who are hired to be police officers simply are not capable of doing the job. They lack the requisite skills, personal commitment to hard work,

Box 12-1

The Positive Power of Training and Retraining

"The secret of the chief's success in moral matters was in his use of the policemen's appetite for understanding. He extended the duration of the academy course for recruits ... he created a series of courses for sergeants, lieutenants, jailers, communications dispatchers, the vice squad, personnel interviewers, advanced officers, and field training officers. In batches of twenty men, training incessantly conducted introductory and two-week refresher courses. Discussions, problem sets, simulation, and lectures: the techniques were always changing, but the education never ceased."

"The process was important and was established—argument, exchange of experience, openness, the whetting of the appetite for ideas, the recognition of problems, and the time for detached reflection. Training was the administration's successful attempt to respond to the moral matters in men's hearts. Training dealt as much with the moral as with the intellectual perplexities of being a policeman. Without a feeling that the world mattered, policemen often surrendered to the worst effects of the paradoxes of power. The Training Division, however, provided the motives, the tools, the stimulation, and the sanctuary busy men needed to get perspective on their lives, to redefine purposes, to challenge old assumptions, and to become morally creative. The effect was profound."

—William K. Muir, Jr., *Police: Streetcorner Politicians*

and integrity to be good officers. In short, they lack the character necessary to get the job done.

If this is the case, then we can hardly expect positive change and we can hardly require such individuals to become the competent professionals that we desire and that the job requires. The only thing individuals who are inept can do under such circumstances—and this is hard to expect of anyone—is to accept their limitations and remove themselves from police work.

Some ineptitude is the product of poor training. Under such circumstances, police officers who possess the requisite skills to accomplish their multiple tasks in the field have simply not been given the education necessary to do so. While it is again difficult to expect this level of self-analysis from any person, such officers must be able to see their shortcomings and have the character to seek training and help to improve. As discussed in depth in our discussions about character, taking a self-critical view of one's personal abilities as a professional may be extremely difficult. But such introspection is an important part of personal character. The intelligent person realizes and deals honestly with his or her shortcomings. It is critical that those entrusted with the powers and responsibilities of being police officers possess this ability to be self-critical and to acknowledge that no one "knows it all." Seeking additional training to erase personal deficiencies can only occur if a person is willing to understand that the job of becoming a competent officer involves an ongoing commitment to grow as a good person.

Some ineptitude is the product of laziness. Police officers, like those involved in any occupation, sometimes become bored and unmotivated. Police work is a profession that is particularly prone to produce "burnout." It is always difficult to avoid the natural tendency to "take it easy." Guided by leaders who are committed to teach and to motivate such officers, individuals who fail to get the job done due to slothfulness must recommit themselves to doing their best for their communities. This may, again, seem like asking for the impossible. But becoming complacent, then recommitting, and then becoming complacent again is a cycle into which many people fall in most professions at one time or another. The good news is that it is part of human nature, in the good person, to reinvigorate oneself on an ongoing basis. Again, it is a matter of having good character that a person sees this propensity and takes action accordingly.

Thus, ineptitude presents us with a new set of problems. First, inept officers need to be able to appreciate their own shortcomings and then to seek out and to be given the best training and counseling possible. Unlike the case of police crime, for example, where culpability clearly rests with the individual officer (unless a systematic, department-wide propensity to behave criminally is present), police administrators must share the responsibility for police ineptitude. The presumption, in other words, must be that officers who fail to do the job because they lack the necessary education, motivation, and skills need to be better educated, trained, and lead. While this will not always be the case, it must be the first assumption. Thus, unlike other types of misconduct, ineptitude involves the shared responsibility of police administrators and leaders. Police leaders must have the character to commit themselves to doing their jobs; teaching and motivating erring officers.

Second, solutions to police ineptitude, unless it is the type of misconduct that involves terminal deficiencies, must be attempted in a positive, retraining atmosphere. This involves a partnership. On one side are police officers who are willing to explore their own shortcomings and to work toward change. On the other side are leaders who are willing to do their jobs and teach appropriate behavior. Such solutions must involve allowing the individual officer to learn and to reorganize his or her view of the job. Leaders must "bend over backwards," in some sense, to expect erring officers to attempt to change in an honest way. Individual officers must confront their own lack of ability and must have the character to commit themselves, with the help of their leaders, to change. This involves a commitment to do one of the hardest things in life: criticize oneself and work to be a better person. Again, the ability to do this is one of the essential ingredients of good character.

Third, police ineptitude of certain types cannot be tolerated and must be dealt with swiftly and surely. If an officer simply does not have the intelligence to do the job, he or she must be terminated. If inept officers are so opposed to change that they cannot take responsibility for their own actions, they are not likely to become competent professionals. Furthermore, as we will discuss in section 12-2, "Excessive Force," some people are not meant to be police officers because of personality traits they possess—that they possessed before they were hired. These individuals, who do not and cannot fit into the role of being a competent and professional officer, must be terminated.

12-2 Excessive Force

The use of excessive force by police officers is an ongoing problem that cannot be completely removed from the police experience because the nature of the job involves using force against people on a regular basis. (See box 12-3.) When this is done, sometimes it will be done inappropriately for one reason or another. Sometimes too much force will be used, sometimes too little. Police work is not an exact science. In fact, it is more of a craft or an art form, and when people attempt to do it perfectly they will fail, as human beings often do.

We are not saying the police must use excessive force to accomplish their tasks. The term "excessive force" means what it says—excessive force. While the police are licensed to use force and must do so sometimes in the interests of beneficence and of justice, they must not use more force than is absolutely necessary to accomplish this task. To use more force than is absolutely necessary is unacceptable and involves a type of police misconduct that is particularly prone to generate hatred in the community and a lack of respect for the police and for the criminal justice system.

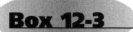

Box 12-3

The Causes of Excessive Force

- Inadequate training in defensive tactics, law, and behavior control.
- The Dirty Harry Problem.
- Personal prejudice.

Excessive force presents a particularly difficult problem for our analysis because it is the product of several dynamics and can be placed in several places in our typology of police misconduct. Some excessive force, as we discussed in the chapter 11, is the product of Dirty Harry-like thinking. That is, sometimes police officers use force to punish offenders on the street for the misdeeds that they have committed. These officers deal out curbside justice because they believe it is their duty to do so.

Such noble cause corruption is based on the notion that the criminal justice system's procedures will not deter and/or punish criminal behavior and thus the police are (they believe) left no alternative but to deter and to punish using their own powers of physical intimidation. We have already dealt with the reasons why this form of police behavior is unacceptable in our noble cause corruption discussion (see chapter 11).

But some excessive force is not aimed at such "noble goals" as deterring crime and punishing guilty offenders. Some excessive force is the product of poor training in defensive techniques and in the law. Some officers use force inappropriately because they do not have enough schooling in how to accomplish their task without doing so, using "come-along" holds and so forth. Equally, some officers use force when none is needed due to misunderstanding the law regarding when they can and cannot make arrests. Each of these types of excessive force is avoidable if proper training and leadership are present.

But a more troublesome reality is that some police excessive force is the product of personal prejudice and nastiness. That is, some excessive force happens because individual officers are prejudiced toward certain types of people and/or are vindictive and even vicious individuals. Police officers sometimes beat up blacks, Hispanics, Asians, white "rednecks," or homosexuals simply because they don't like those kinds of people. Thus, some citizens become the victims of police abuse due to their personal characteristics and not due to having done something that is illegal.

This does not happen as often as it used to, but it does occur. When it does, there is no alternative to terminating the guilty officer(s). There is not much we can say here, in a book about being a good person and a good police officer, that speaks to people who act upon these types of prejudices. They do not belong in police work, and they must be eliminated. No amount of discussion can effectively change a genuinely vicious person who likes to hurt people and/or who hates certain types of people into a person of good character.

However, while those few police officers who are genuinely vicious and brutal must be taken off the force, we must finish this brief discussion of excessive force by saying something about racism, religious prejudice, homophobia, and sexism. We do not wish to suggest here that being a competent, professional police officer necessarily entails having a personality that is totally without prejudice. Very few people (in fact, one may argue, no human beings) live their lives without developing some prejudices about groups of people. Race prejudice, religious prejudice, sex prejudice, and sexual-orientation prejudice are just some examples of the types of ideas that many if not most of us carry with us in our hearts and minds.

Such pre-judgments about groups of people are created within us in many ways. We obtain them from our parents, from our peers, from our social institutions, from the media, and so on. It is unrealistic to think people will not possess at least some of these ideas in their world views. As human beings, we cannot expect police officers to be saints.

But having said this, it is important to point out what we can expect of police officers. What we can and do expect of competent, professional officers is that they will carry such prejudicial notions inside them and not behave in such a way as to allow these ideas to influence their behavior as cops. We do not care what police officers think about various groups of people as long as those thoughts do not determine how they behave as officers. In attempting to keep an eye on one's own prejudices, competent officers acknowledge they are not perfect and realize they must take great care to keep prejudice out of their professional decision making.

Is this possible? Can people hold private prejudices and avoid using them professionally? Of course they can. All competent professionals who deal with the public on a regular basis—be they doctors, lawyers, welfare workers, teachers, or police officers—can work consciously at keeping their personal prejudices out of their professional decision making. It is not only possible to do this, but we have every right to demand that it is done.

Thus, police officers of good character are always on guard to take care that their own prejudices do not creep into their on-duty behavior. With regard to the use of force, competent and professional police officers will always be circumspect when they use force against people they personally dislike. In using force, in making arrest/no arrest decisions, or in solving people's order-maintenance-oriented problems, police officers need to help one another in this effort. They must always be aware that their roles are not being played out appropriately if they fall into the curbside justice mode and treat people differently because of their characteristics rather than their behavior.

12-3 Personal Misconduct

All Americans possess certain constitutionally protected rights to privacy. When, if ever, are these individual rights denied to police officers? Under what circumstances does a police officer's off-duty, personal behavior become the business of the police department and/or the public? More specifically, when does a police officer's off-duty personal misconduct become something that is relevant to the job on duty? See box 12-4.

There is no simple answer to the question posed in box 12-4. Off-duty, personal misbehavior can cease to be one's own business and can become the concern of police accountability systems and even the public in several ways. The analytical problem is that personal misconduct exists on a sort of sliding scale. Sometimes it becomes publicized and important; other times it remains private and unimportant. There are several levels of concern for us in our consideration of personal misconduct.

12-3a Off-Duty Crime

The first and most obvious example of personal misconduct of concern to us is police off-duty crime. When a police officer is arrested off duty for shoplifting, for example, this invariably makes headlines and becomes the business of police accountability systems. Because the police are licensed to arrest others for criminal behavior, such off-duty conduct is obviously not a personal matter, as it could arguably be with other professionals. If, for example, a doctor were to be guilty of income tax evasion, it would not necessarily follow that this misconduct impacts his or her ability to minister to people's sickness and injury. But because of the role the police perform, their off-duty crime cannot be ignored and cannot be treated as irrelevant, personal business.

Box 12-4

What Is "Personal" and What Is "Professional" Behavior?

In 1998 and 1999, President Bill Clinton was embroiled in a scandal that eventually lead to his impeachment. While he was acquitted of the charges leveled against him, the scandal was taken seriously by his political enemies and by the mainstream media. The scandal involved the president having a sexual affair with a young intern in the White House.

Throughout the nearly two years the scandal played out, opinion polls taken over and over again indicated a large majority of Americans did not care about it. Several pollsters interviewed people about this dynamic, and what these citizens said is important for our discussion here. It turns out that while most people thought the president's actions were disgusting and/or unacceptable, they saw such sexual behavior as an issue of "personal conduct" that did not disqualify Clinton from being president.

Thus, while people did not like his actions, they said it was not the business of the country but a personal matter between the president and his family.

What do you think? What would you think if the transgressor were not president of the United States but a police officer? Would such marital infidelity disqualify a person from being a cop, or is it an issue of personal, private business?

When it becomes public knowledge due to the arrest of a police officer, police off-duty crime immediately becomes the concern of everyone who cares about police officer ethics. But sometimes such crime does not get publicized. This can happen because the local media help to keep things quiet. Or police officers can be involved in off-duty crime and not be caught. Or they might be caught and not arrested/prosecuted. While it might not be fair to individual officers, a sliding scale exists wherein that which gets publicized must be treated seriously and that which does not can (often) be avoided. This is a practical reality of "how things work in the world" that may or may not be the way we would want them to work.

For the purposes of our discussion of police ethics, we must be concerned with all police off-duty crime. But for the reasons just suggested, we have to weigh the issue of the relative level of gravity of police off-duty crime. Are police officers who receive off-duty speeding tickets to be disciplined on the job? What about parking tickets? How much are we to be concerned with the ethical dilemma of officers arresting others for what they themselves have done if the crimes committed are petty and minor?

Are we not expecting police officers to be saints if we consider every minor offense to be some sort of indication of their character—or lack of it?

One might be prone to answer this question by saying that infractions, crimes punishable only by fines and not imprisonment, should be excluded from our concern here. But what if a police officer develops a pronounced pattern of driving violations that indicate a lack of respect for the law? What if an officer obtains twenty moving violations or one hundred parking tickets? Could (or should) we be concerned about such offenses, even though they are minor in a legal sense?

The answer is that there is no answer. There is no one way to analyze what should be of concern to students of police ethics. We will only briefly outline the following rule.

> Police officer off-duty crime is of concern to us all the time if it is felonious and/or violent in nature, some of the time if it is of the misdemeanor type, and seldom if it is infraction related. Then too, any pattern of criminal behavior can be troublesome, no matter how minor the infractions involved.

12-3b Duty-Related Misconduct

A second way in which personal misconduct becomes the business of the department/public is when, no matter how private it might be, the behavior can logically be said to impact directly upon the ability of the police officers to perform their duties. For example, when an officer is found to have an alcoholism problem, such a problem is (arguably) not the sort that can be left at home when the officer shows up for work. That is, alcoholism carries with it certain dynamics that cannot be divorced from the work-a-day life of a police officer. Alcoholics can suffer from withdrawal symptoms when denied their drug; they can have functional problems relating to decision making and motor skills; and they can be prone to pursue drinking ("just one drink" is often rationalized) when working.

Thus, we have suggested alcoholism is a personal problem that has such far-reaching ramifications it cannot be ignored by anyone who seeks to evaluate the character of an alcoholic officer. A similar argument can be made with respect to officers who are involved in domestic abuse, marital infidelity, drug problems, and violence of any kind in their off-duty lives. While any and all of these types of problems can become legal issues, that is to say criminal in their nature, often they don't. Often the drug user is not caught, the domestic abuser is not arrested, the bar fighter is not prosecuted, and so on.

When these dynamics present themselves in the lives of average citizens, civilians are often left alone by the criminal justice system. We argue here that when such problems come to light in the lives of police officers, whether or not they become criminal in their nature is irrelevant. Such behavior cannot remain private because of how directly it relates to the abilities of the officers to perform their duties on the job. Thus, we are suggesting that officers who have such problems receive the type of counseling and/or rehabilitation that is necessary to diminish if not solve these difficulties. We are also saying that no amount of rationalizing can divorce these types of personal problems from an evaluation of the officer's on-the-job competence and ethical perspective.

12-4 Character Revisited

We cannot finish this discussion of what sort of behavior is the cop's private business and what type is of universal concern without referring back to our discussions about character (see chapters 3 and 4). In a real sense, everything police officers do at any time in their lives indicates what kind of people they are and thus paints a picture of their character. Nothing—no matter how private or personal—can be left out of our analysis of a person's (police officer's) character.

As surely as character determines one's competence as a professional, it is fashioned and exhibited in everything we do every day. Thus, we might suggest that nothing in the life of a powerful agent of the state (police officer) is personal and private. That, of course, is an unacceptable idea to us as Americans accustomed to constitutional protections regarding privacy. But it does give us food for thought regarding how the competent professional must approach this issue of personal misconduct.

The professional police officer, concerned with character and with the marriage between ethics and competence in the way this book suggests ought to be the case, should be constantly vigilant with regard to his or her own personal behavior. We are our own consciences, in this sense, and nothing and no one outside of our own souls should be remotely as important to us as are our own evaluations of who we are and how we ought to act.

"In this life, you don't have to prove anything to anyone but yourself."

— A friend's admonition to a Notre Dame football player in the movie *Rudy*

Thus, the modern, professional police officer must be held by himself or herself to a high standard of behavior both on and off duty. Professional officers are constantly circumspect about their personal and work-a-day lives in a way that keeps their actions above reproach—always, every day, under all circumstances.

Summary

In this chapter, we have wrestled with two thorny issues. We have moved away from analyzing types of police misconduct that are obviously unacceptable and have discussed misconduct that is either inadvertent or to some extent shielded from view due to its personal, private nature. In some sense, we have entered a world where the most important issues of police ethics reside. That is, when discussing ineptitude and personal, off-duty conduct, we engage individual police officers with concerns about how they must observe, analyze, and control their own worst impulses.

Here, in this set of discussions, we have most directly confronted the central point of our entire book: In the end, police officers are most importantly accountable to themselves. No regulatory system of outside controls, no discipline that is imposed from elsewhere, and no supervisory oversight can be substituted for the internal, socialized ethics of the individual officer. Professional police officers carry with them an ethical framework that controls their worst impulses to be self-centered and vindictive and ennobles their efforts to be fair and just.

We now turn, in Part 4, to discuss how all of this comes together. First we will analyze the Law Enforcement Code of Ethics, the consummate statement of how police officers ought to act. Then, we will discuss the entire package of our character-related discussion and consider who police officers ought to be.

Topics for Discussion

1. The authors suggest police officers need to have a commitment to the development of their own competencies that allows them to be able to analyze their own strengths and weaknesses. Think about your own training. Ask yourself, "In what areas of study and training am I most lacking? In what areas do I need to expand? What information do I need

to obtain to most effectively pursue my preparation to become the best officer I can be?" Can you discuss these points of self-analysis?

2. What is "excessive force"? Police officers are supposed to use "only that force which is absolutely necessary to overcome illegal force." What does that mean? Discuss how troublesome it is to have no specific, concrete definitions to help us in analyzing the use of appropriate force.

3. Refer to box 12-4. Because the impeachment of President Clinton was such a well-reported event, most readers will have an opinion about what happened. Do you agree with a majority of Americans—that what he did was unethical but it did not relate to the job he was doing as president? Relate this discussion to police officer personal misconduct.

Part

Part

4

Implications

Chapter 13
The Law
Enforcement
Code of Ethics

Chapter 14
On Becoming
a Good Officer

In chapters 13 and 14, we will use all that we have discussed to accomplish two tasks. First, in chapter 13 ("The Law Enforcement Code of Ethics") we will relate our ethic to the code of ethics that has underwritten the practice of police work for many years. We will find that while it has its critics, it is a thoughtful, educated, and professional code of conduct that is of practical utility for those in police service on the street every day.

Second, in chapter 14 ("On Becoming a Good Officer") we will engage in a discussion of how the contemporary professional officer can actively work at developing an ethics-based competence to be effective as a proactive member of today's police force. These will be critical discussions for the thoughtful reader.

13

The Law Enforcement Code of Ethics

"Any officer who takes this [Law Enforcement Code of Ethics] seriously will quickly learn that he cannot do what the code seems to require. He will then either have to quit the force or consign its mandates to Code Heaven."
— Michael Davis, Criminologist

Outline

Most professions have a code of ethics, and police work is no exception. This chapter will analyze the Law Enforcement Code of Ethics (see box 13-1) and apply our ethical perspective to its tenets. We will see that various schools of thought regarding what it means to be a good person, a good police officer, and to do good works in life are all included in the ideas and ideals embodied in the code. Along the way, we will discuss some criticisms of the code that suggest it is unrealistic and, therefore, might do more harm than good. Finally, we will argue that the code, with its somewhat vague, general, and idealistic construction, is an important focal point for any serious police officer who seeks to become the consummate professional.

13-1 The Tone of the Code of Ethics

There are several different types of codes of ethics, ranging from the specific to the general in their approaches to defining appropriate conduct for professionals. At the most specific or practical level, some codes are like police departmental general order manuals. That is, they provide mandatory sets of rules, usually very long and complicated, which serve as the basis upon which discipline is meted out when professionals misbehave. Such codes are practical in the sense that they attempt to present specific, how-to-do-it type rules for day-to-day professional life. They are impractical, however, due to their unwieldy, complicated, voluminous nature. They are "just too big to handle."

The second type of code provides general statements of principles or guidelines that present values for an organization. Many police departments and organizations of all kinds, private and public, have these sets of guidelines. Some of these codes are elaborate, expanded "mission statements." They are attempts to give organizations long-range rather than immediate, short-term goals at which to aim. They are less specific than general orders but more organization-focused.

The third type of code of ethics is the "aspirational" code. This type constructs an ideal model of what the profession should be like and how the professional should behave. The Law Enforcement Code of Ethics is such a code. It has its critics precisely because it is not specific and is, instead, idealistic and general. Yet its strength lies in just this idealism. The specifics of how one behaves as a police officer and of how one handles various types of details are so complicated and variable that any attempt to categorize them is doomed to failure. As is the case with general order manuals, lists for police officers consisting of what to do and what not to do are so voluminous they are almost worthless. No one could read, study, understand and completely memorize them.

Box 13-1

The Law Enforcement Code of Ethics

As a Law Enforcement Officer my fundamental duty is to serve mankind; to safeguard lives and property; to protect the innocent against deception, the weak against oppression or intimidation, and the peaceful against violence of disorder; and to respect the Constitutional Rights of all men to liberty, equality, and justice.

I will keep my private life unsullied as an example to all; maintain courageous calm in the face of danger, scorn, or ridicule; develop self-restraint, and be constantly mindful of the welfare of others. Honest in thought and deed in both my personal and official life, I will be exemplary in obeying the laws of the land and the regulations of my department. Whatever I see or hear of a confidential nature or that is confided to me in my official capacity will be kept ever secret unless revelation is necessary in the performance of my duty.

I will never act officiously or permit personal feelings, prejudices, animosities, or friendship to influence my decision. With no compromise for crime and with relentless prosecution of criminals, I will enforce the law courteously and appropriately without fear or favor, malice or ill will, never employing unnecessary force or violence and never accepting gratuities.

I recognize the badge of my office as a symbol of public faith, and I accept it as a public trust to be held so long as I am true to the ethics of the police service. I will constantly strive to achieve these objectives and ideals, dedicating myself before God to my chosen profession ... law enforcement.

Thus, The Law Enforcement Code of Ethics, aiming as it does to construct an idealized vision of how the competent and ethical professional should be and behave, is an important code of the aspirational type. It sets general guidelines and presents ethical tenets toward which the professional should aim. Understanding that no one is a saint under the pressure of life on the street as a cop, the code suggests an ideal at which all competence-seeking, professional police officers ought to aim in both their private and professional lives.

Let us consider the specifics of the code and analyze how what it suggests parallels several ethical perspectives.

13-2 The Code and Ethical Perspectives

One of the complications and paradoxes of police work is that no one set of classical, ethical principles is always applicable to every situation and to every moment's challenges. Our discussion has included three ethical perspectives. We have treated Kant's ethical formalism, Mill's utilitarianism, and our own ethic to live by, which is a combination of the other two. We will discuss all three of them here.

13-2a Ethical Formalism

The Law Enforcement Code of Ethics presents numerous principles that logically fit into the perspective of ethical formalism. In a Kantian sense, the code suggests that some principles by which police officers ought to live are absolute. No amount of rationalization, before or after the fact, can (or should) be used to explain away or to make excuses about police officer behavior that transgresses these principles. Examples of these absolute principles are included in box 13-2. It behooves us to consider an example from these principles to illustrate what we mean when we say they represent absolute rules of conduct.

In chapter 10, we discussed Kania's idea that the acceptance of small gratuities by police officers might be a good thing. The familiar and friendly relationship that might develop between police officer and gift giver would be good for developing the type of bonds between police and citizens that community-based policing is all about.

In asking the police officer to vow to avoid taking any gratuities whatsoever, the code asserts that the acceptance of any gifts involves a dereliction of the officer's duty. No matter how small the gift might be, the code suggests that—in a Kantian, absolutist sense—when an officer accepts any gratuity, he or she makes a moral judgment that sacrifices the authority of the badge in the name of favoritism.

The absolute statement against taking gratuities rejects utilitarianism. It reminds us about the slippery slope idea that small gratuities can lead to larger ones, that grass eating leads to meat eating (see chapter 10). The code rejects Kania's suggestion that some small gratuities should be ignored and accepts the argument that any gift carries with it the assumption of future, reciprocal favors. If free coffee is given to a police officer merely because the coffee-giver is in a good mood and feels a sense of community and not because the coffee-giver expects any future potential favor, then why is free coffee not given out to everyone? Free cups of coffee mean something, the code suggests; and no matter what they mean to the coffee-giver, they cannot be accepted by the police officer.

Box 13-2

Ethical Formalism: Absolute Rules of Police Conduct

The code includes several elements or principles that can be considered absolutist in their content:

- I will be exemplary in obeying the laws of the land and the regulations of my department.

- I will never act officiously or permit personal feelings, prejudices, animosities or friendships to influence my decisions.

- I will enforce the law courteously and appropriately without fear or favor, malice or ill will.

- I will never accept gratuities.

The code's logic here may seem too rigid and judgmental to some. But this is precisely the strength of the Kantian approach. It presents duties and responsibilities that are absolute and not open to debate. It thus creates a code of behavior that is unassailable, not subject to interpretation, not open to be manipulated in light of what someone (or anyone) considers the practical realities of particular circumstances. Ethical formalism is, thus, the friend of the rule of law. We know from earlier discussions that deviants use any number of ways to rationalize misbehavior. Ethical formalism suggests an absolute set of principles from which there is no escaping into the world of rationalization and excuse making.

Now, applying our ethic to live by, we suggest that the code is correct here and that Kantians, equally, are correct. To accept any gratuity is to create a future situation that involves favoritism. This flies in the face of our principle of applying justice equitably. Even a free cup of coffee can create in the police officer/citizen interaction of the future a dynamic that is troublesome (see box 13-3). With regard to free coffee or half-priced food in particular, why do it? Why create such a problem in the first place?

13-2b Utilitarianism

The rest of the examples in box 13-2 are equally absolutist in their content. But there is more in the code. Its pronouncements also include principles that are clearly utilitarian. (Both act utilitarianism and rule utilitarianism are in evidence in the code.) With regard to our ethic to live by, these tenets of the code ask the professional officer to think about the

Box 13-3

The Trouble with "Little" Gratuities

A restaurant in a violent and crime-ridden area provided local police officers with free cups of coffee and half-priced food whenever they showed
up. This, the owners and operators reasoned, kept the police around and
was good insurance against being robbed. Indeed, the place sat in the
middle of the highest crime area in the county and was never robbed or
burgled.

One night after closing, the cook of the restaurant was stopped on his
way home by several of the officers who benefited from this practice. He
was drunk, very drunk, driving all over the road in an extremely dangerous manner. What were the officers to do? This man was a sort of "patron"
to the officers, having given them substantial "gifts" over the years. They
were in an awkward situation. While the man was not arrested, the two
officers involved resolved never to go to the restaurant again and never to
take free food or coffee again because of the situation in which they had
been placed.

In making this decision, these officers were showing the good
character that it takes to question one's perspective and behavior. They
were acting as competent professionals, completely in tune with our ethic
to live by.

principle of beneficence. Specifically, they are about doing good and preventing or eliminating evil.

Box 13-4 exhibits examples of the code's act utilitarianism relating to
specific situations—asking officers to focus on those citizens immediately
involved in details on the street. Clearly, one of the most important charges
all police officers must undertake is to "protect the peaceful against violence or disorder." But what this principle means and how one might go
about attempting to attain it on the street present the police officer with a
complicated, variable set of concerns and tactics.

Who are "the peaceful"? This is not always clear. Are "the peaceful"
those citizens who want quiet to prevail on a Saturday night in their
neighborhoods? If so, then are partygoers in some sense criminals or, at
the very least, people who mean to do harm and create disorder? In celebration of the turn of the year, are not New Year's Eve revelers decent, law-
abiding citizens? Do they not have the right, on such an occasion, to make
some noise, dance and play, drink and cavort, and so on?

Box 13-4

Act Utilitarianism—Responding to Specific Situations

The Law Enforcement Code of Ethics includes the following principles that should be considered variable in that they require police officers to take into account the numerous ramifications of taking action in specific cases. Police officers should always attempt to calculate the consequences of different potential solutions to everyday problems as they seek to:

- Safeguard lives and property.
- Protect the innocent against deception.
- Protect the weak against oppression or intimidation.
- Protect the peaceful against violence or disorder.
- Maintain courage in the face of danger, scorn, or ridicule.

In considering what do about a loud party call on New Year's Eve, officers must strike a balance. Utilitarianism tells us these balances will not always look the same and the appropriate police actions to be taken will not always take the same form. If called to suppress the noise of a New Year's party, police officers may very well tend to leave the partiers alone and even to explain to the complaining party that "this is one of those times when making noise and cavorting is appropriate." Equally applicable, if a loud party is occurring in a college town on the night of the big football victory, the police may be understandably reluctant to challenge the rights of the Saturday night noisemakers.

But if a loud party takes place on a Tuesday night, a school night and a work night, doesn't the formula change? Isn't it true that the same people making exactly the same amount of noise in exactly the same place might be guilty of disturbing the peace on a Tuesday night when they were not guilty of it on a Saturday night? Common sense and utilitarian logic say these are two completely different situations. The competent, professional police officer needs to understand this, to act accordingly, and to be comfortable with the fact that there is not one appropriate, legal, ethical rule for dealing with loud parties that fits all conditions and all occasions.

Focusing on the specific circumstances of the individual incident, police officers, operating as utilitarians, have to acknowledge that what is fair, just, and (even) legal in dealing with such details will never be quite the same. This is true even though their charge to "protect the peaceful from violence and disorder" must always be taken seriously and acted upon. Our ethic to live by, which includes this utilitarian idea, suggests that on such occasions genuine "harm" is not at issue. But "doing good" is. It is one of the multiple roles of the police to help people to pursue good in their lives and to allow them, whenever possible, the individual responsibility to make choices. When "merely" loud noise is at issue, such a situation is present.

In chapter 6, we differentiated between two types of utilitarianism. The Law Enforcement Code of Ethics includes both. Recall that rule utilitarianism involves variable tactics and outcomes that are not as closely related to the specific incidents presented to the police officer as act utilitarianism is. That is, while rule utilitarianism shares with act utilitarianism a lack of absolutism, it nevertheless is different because it focuses on the long-term implications of police decision making. When police officers conduct themselves as rule utilitarians, they make decisions—that may differ from time to time, place to place, and circumstance to circumstance—that focus on the importance of the consequences for society if all police officers behaved in the same way all of the time.

Box 13-5 exhibits examples of principles included in the code that exhort individual officers to consider the larger and (again) long-term significance of their decisions on the street (rule utilitarianism).

While not setting absolute principles of conduct (as ethical formalism does), utilitarianism sees police behavior in a broader context. Certainly, no one could argue with the assertion that the police officer has a "fundamental duty to serve mankind." This principle is basic to the police service and is central to our ethic to live by. Anyone who enters police work without this in mind, without this underwriting principle as the central reason for his or her professional commitment, is in the wrong business and should get out. The trials and tribulations of the work-a-day experience, the personal stresses and sacrifices involved, the tests and challenges of police work, all of these are prices not worth paying unless they are underwritten by a commitment to serve humanity, to help people.

But what does such a fundamental duty involve? What does it mean to serve mankind? Police officers make so many decisions that affect people's lives directly that they are consistently challenged to take the broader, long-term interests of people, communities, and justice into account. As we have taken great pains to point out, balances must be struck between the interests of individual citizens. Exactly when, if ever, do the interests of society outweigh those of the individual?

Box 13-5

Rule Utilitarianism—The Long-Term Importance of Individual Details

The Law Enforcement Code of Ethics contains several utilitarian principles that require the police officer to take a broad view of the best interests of the community and of justice in the long run. When making individual decisions regarding choices of action, police officers must remember that:

- My fundamental duty is to serve mankind.

- I must keep my private life unsullied as an example to all.

- I must be honest in thought and deed in both my personal and official lives.

- I recognize the badge of my office as a symbol of public faith, and I accept it as a public trust to be held so long as I am true to the ethics of the police service.

For example, one of the classic questions used (usually by oral board examiners) to confront police officer candidates is, "What would you do if you stopped a drunk driver and found that it was a friend of yours?" This question presents the would-be police officer with an ethical dilemma of the tallest order. While it doesn't happen very often on the street, being confronted with the criminal behavior of a friend or acquaintance does occur. What to do?

Utilitarianism (like our ethic to live by) suggests that in deciding whether or not to make an arrest, officers must consider the long-term interests of justice. If friends are let go, then utilitarianism suggests everyone should be let go. Given the impact drunk driving has on our society (thousands of deaths every year are caused by it), how could an ethical officer live with letting a friend go? The answer is that the ethical officer cannot. Such a decision (to let a drunk driver continue driving) would not only constitute a failure to remove harm (the principle of beneficence), but it would also interfere with the principle that justice ought to be applied equally to all.

So included in our ethic to live by is the utilitarian logic that the long-term implications of making a rule for everyone must be taken into account in a way that protects the interests of all. In the drunk driving example, the ethical officer must either make an arrest or, if time and situation permit, hand the detail over to another officer. In doing this, the officer would be insuring that the law is applied objectively and in an even-handed manner to all.

The vagueness of the Law Enforcement Code of Ethics is so pronounced that there are critics who consider it to be a waste of time. It is toward this discussion of the criticisms of the code that we now turn.

13-3 The Code of Ethics As an "Ideal" or "Target"

Even though the Law Enforcement Code of Ethics is widely accepted as a meaningful set of principles upon which to focus the police officer's career, it has its critics. As criminal ethicist Joycelyn Pollock states, "One argument is that the code specifies such perfect behavior that it is irrelevant to the realities of most officers. The wide disparity between the code and actual behavior is detrimental to the validity and credibility of the code."

Aside from this argument—that it is impossible and impractical to live up to the code—is another that states the code is simply too vague and confusing. It is not specific enough as a how-to-do-it guide, critics say, and merely adds confusion to the problem of the multiple, conflicting, and vague police roles that create some of the central frustrations of police work.

Is this criticism valid? Are we asking too much of police officers that they live by the code's ideals? Is it a waste of time, in the real world, to ask people to do things that are, if not impossible, at least extremely difficult? How do we answer these critics?

From our perspective, these critics miss the point of this or any other code of conduct. Certainly, it is extremely troublesome to expect people operating under the stresses of everyday police work to live up to the code's dictates every day. Even so, why is it a waste of time to ask people to do their best to attempt to live up to such ideals? Isn't it the height of cynicism to give up on trying to behave in an ideal way? Are we saying that because people cannot always be perfect, because they have character flaws, we should avoid asking them to try to be so? Furthermore, isn't it genuinely dangerous to build excuses into the minds of such powerful individuals as police officers? Are we not creating the excuse that because police officers cannot live up to such ideals all of the time it is acceptable for them to behave in whatever fashion they can rationalize—due to the stresses of the job?

What are the implications of giving up on such a code? We believe the long-term ramifications of this type of thinking are devastating for police officers, for citizens, for society, and for justice. For example, because many people find it impossible to avoid driving while drunk, are we to give up on applying that law? Because people cheat on their spouses, are we to give up on the institution of marriage? Because children and adults fail to learn what they should in school, are we to give up on education? And in the grandest scheme of things, because people regularly transgress against all sorts of rules, laws, moral tenets, and ethical principles in life, are we to say that having norms and values of any kind is a waste of time?

Simply because police officers, like all people, are flawed human beings, and because it is impossible to live up to the tenets of the Law Enforcement Code of Ethics all of the time does not give us the go-ahead to abandon the attempt to do so. The reason there are rules, regulations, laws, courts, and prisons is that people fail to behave themselves when left on their own in the first place. If we say to police officers, to ourselves, that we may use the excuse that we are imperfect human beings to rationalize not even trying to be moral individuals, then more than the ethics of police officers are at stake. Such a cynical approach to ethics allows that setting up standards of conduct, being impossible to live by all of the time as they are, is an exercise in futility. If this were the case, then society and all human institutions are complete wastes of time.

The Law Enforcement Code of Ethics encompasses an important set of principles, defines an ideal conceptualization of what a police officer ought to be, and sets up a goal toward which all honest, hardworking, dedicated professionals can aim. As such, it is or ought to be a critical part of the life of every police officer everywhere.

Summary

In chapter 13, we have gone back to our two classical schools of thought about ethics and shown how they are included in our ethic to live by. We have taken the Law Enforcement Code of Ethics apart, to some extent, and discussed how our composite ethic, an ethic to live by, applies to different sorts of ethical questions faced by police officers on a regular basis. Our examples are commonplace and not obscure by any means. And in working through this process, we have attempted to indicate that the ethic to live by from chapter 7 is an appropriate, measured, logical way to approach ethical decision making in police work.

Equally, we have dissected the Law Enforcement Code of Ethics and shown that it is a well constructed, although vague, set of principles that translates the two principles of the ethic to live by into a larger set of general tenets. Finally, we have discussed criticisms of the code and suggested that critics miss the point, the strength of the code. We grant that it is vague and not full of specific "rules of the road," but given the multiple, conflicting, and vague roles the police have to play on the street, the code is a good attempt at presenting our ethic to live by in more concrete terms.

No one dealing with the stresses and dilemmas of police work will be able to live up to its tenets completely all of the time. But the Law Enforcement Code of Ethics is an important target at which all competent professionals can direct their efforts to live up to the principles of beneficence and justice.

Topics for Discussion

1. Read and discuss the Law Enforcement Code of Ethics, taking particular note of how vague its pronouncements are. What does it tell us about how to act as police officers and what does it leave to our own imaginations and ethical perspectives?
2. Discuss the text's example of confronting a drunk driving friend while on duty. What would you do? What should you do? Apply Kant, Mill, and our ethic to live by to the dilemma presented to you by the competing duties to "stick by a friend" and to apply the law justly.
3. Critics point out that the differences between the code's dictates and the "real world" of police work are great. Discuss both the strengths and the weaknesses of the code's lack of realism.

Chapter 14

On Becoming a Good Officer

> *"Police work is just common sense. Any good person can become a good police officer."*
>
> - Skip Stevens, Retired Police Officer

Outline

As our introductory quote from an experienced police officer indicates, there is nothing magical about becoming a good police officer. Good officers are not in any sense "born" into this world. Any good, hard-working, honest person with the requisite physical abilities and intelligence can become a competent professional if he or she is willing to work at it. Chapter 14 discusses how a person might approach that task—the job of becoming a competent professional—in the face of all of the stresses, opportunities for failure, and ethical dilemmas presented by life on the street in uniform.

14-1 Education: The Importance of the Liberal Arts

Psychologist Lawrence Kohlberg studied the development over time of morals and ethical thinking. He found that people go through certain stages in putting together an increasingly sophisticated understanding of morals. After several decades of studying moral development, Kohlberg made some specific suggestions (summarized in box 14-1) about how ethical thinking could be encouraged.

When looking at the list in box 14-1, it seems to be an argument supporting the utility of a broadly based college education. While Kohlberg didn't specifically refer either to college or to police officers, for the purposes of our discussion the idea that a liberal arts education is important for the development of police professionalism is central.

The experience of taking college classes, whether or not one goes to college with the intention of obtaining a degree, is good for police officers for two reasons. The first flows directly from Kohlberg's list. It has to do with the historical rationale for obtaining a broadly based, liberal arts education in general. The second reason college is good for cops relates more directly to the specific facts and theories one can learn there. Put more succinctly, the two sets of reasons why a college experience is important for the competent professional are process-oriented and substance-oriented.

As Kohlberg seems to be telling us, the process-oriented reasons for including the college experience in the life of the professional police officer have to do with engendering an appreciation for moral thinking. Kohlberg's list suggests it is good to have practice in taking other people's points of view, in confronting ethical dilemmas, in questioning one's own ways of thinking, in arguing logically, and so on. What these experiences amount to are, in a procedural sense, what the college experience is all about. Going to lectures, taking notes, studying them, reading books with varying points of view, getting into debates in the classroom and over coffee, writing papers wherein you take a stance and defend it logically—all

Box 14-1

Kohlberg's Ideas for Encouraging Moral Growth

Psychologist Lawrence Kohlberg described the following criteria as being necessary for moral growth. Being exposed to these types of experiences expands the individual's ethical understanding and thus helps to engender professionalism:

- Being in situations where seeing things from other points of view is encouraged.
- Engaging in logical thinking.
- Having the responsibility to make moral decisions and to influence one's own moral world.
- Being exposed to moral controversy and thus to ambiguity.
- Being exposed to the reasoning of an individual whose moral thinking is more sophisticated than one's own.
- Participating in creating and maintaining a just community.

of these things are what college is about. People who experience them are participating in the ongoing creation of their own increasingly sophisticated points of view, the expansion of their perspectives on life, and the enhancement of their personal ethical frames of reference. Thus, this is one way in which people improve their character.

Wrestling with other people's points of view is something police officers do every day on the street. Facing up to ethical dilemmas and making the right choices are skills that can be improved with practice. Understanding that life on the street is full of ambiguities and being comfortable living with them are equally life-process-oriented skills that can be enhanced in any individual. Participating in democratic and semidemocratic community development is the essence of the modern community-based policing officer's role. Kohlberg's entire list of experiences involves practicing skills and honing abilities that are directly relevant to the process involved in successfully policing a beat in a competent and professional manner.

Thus, a critical part of developing professionalism is going through the kind of intellectual experience college involves. But there is more. The college experience involves more than merely being around and intermingling with people who hold other points of view and who have different experiences in life. There is a great deal of substantive learning college can bring to any individual that helps to engender professional competence in the police officer. This is the substance-oriented reason for going to college.

Modern college programs in criminal justice and law expose students to practical knowledge that is of great importance. Some topics have direct, day-to-day relevance for the police officer's participation in the criminal justice system. Classes on forensics, interrogation, search and seizure, and law are but a few examples of practical areas of expertise that can be expanded in the classroom. The competence of the police professional can be greatly enhanced by continuous exposure to cutting-edge theory and practice in these important police-related fields.

But exposure to the liberal arts includes far more than such practical courses. To become a competent officer, the individual can benefit from any number of courses of study that might appear at first glance to be only remotely related to the job of policing the streets. Developing a well rounded, broadly based understanding of history, psychology, sociology, and political science—to name but a few subject areas—is of critical importance to creating a genuinely educated and integrated individual. See box 14-2.

It makes good sense to understand the broad sweep of American history, beginning with the colonial experience and the struggle for independence. Understanding how and why the Revolutionary War was fought gives the officer a feeling for the central ideals of America, such as limited government and individual rights, that are underwritten by our institutions and our treasured historical documents. The Declaration of Independence, the Constitution, the Bill of Rights, and the Gettysburg Address all speak about American ideals that offer important insights into being a police officer.

Understanding the history of slavery and the Civil War, the two World Wars, the labor movement, the civil rights movement, and even more recent events, such as the feminist and gay rights movements, will give officers an important perspective. This perspective helps them to understand the concerns of any number of different types of citizens they regularly encounter on the street. The study of the history of policing undertaken in most criminal justice programs can help a contemporary officer to understand just what community-based policing is all about. This in turn helps officers deal with the changing expectations with which people confront police officers today.

Psychology courses on abnormal psychology, on personality development and disorders, on adolescent psychology, and on individual tech-

Box 14-2

Reasons for Police Officers to go to College

- To experience interactions with different types of people, points of view, ideas and ideals, and to practice questioning one's own perspective.

- To learn specific subject matter related directly to police work and related in general to the development of an understanding of culture and American institutions.

- To expose officers to "other-than-police-subcultural" perspectives on life.

niques for rationalizing deviance all help to create a broad understanding of the human experience. In sociology, students learn about the creation of norms and values, about the dynamics of subcultures, about diverse cultural experiences and expectations, and about deviance in particular. All of this is good because it expands an officer's ability to be competent in dealing with diverse people and with the complicated dynamics that create both deviance and normality in the world.

In political science, students learn about American institutions, about how change occurs in the law, about the place of the courts, legislatures and the police in our complicated system of governance. The multiple stresses and conflicting goals and roles of the American police can create frustration in the modern officer who does not possess an understanding of these subjects. Ignorance of these topics can make an officer prone toward Dirty Harry-type cynicism. This in turn can make effective policing impossible.

Thus, Kohlberg asks us to engage the central reason for obtaining an education—that the learned individual possesses a certain wide-ranging understanding of life, of the human experience, of their society, and of its institutions and history. This learning creates in the individual the ability to go about the job of policing, of moralizing for others, and of making life-changing decisions for them using a foundation that integrates intelligence, problem-solving abilities, substantive learning, knowledge about the real world, and insightful intuition.

This laundry list of reasons for experiencing at least some college courses is powerful enough in itself. But there is one more important reason for officers to be involved in ongoing educational experiences throughout the course of their lives in uniform. As we have discussed in several places, the police subculture is a powerful entity that can give an officer support and a sense of belonging. But membership in such a subculture can also have its drawbacks.

Spending most if not all of one's time with members of a single-minded group can make any individual narrow, limited, and stilted in his or her view of life and approach to problem solving. Such experience can convince a person that there is only one way to see the world, to think about life, to live and enjoy life, and to define the good in life. Because it is a basic principle of our diverse American culture that none of these things is true, spending time in such an exclusive club can have terrible consequences for the interests of justice on the street, given that "the police are the law."

Thus, continued experiences in the world of ideas and the give-and-take of intellectual life, coupled with ongoing interactions with people who are not members of the police subculture, can have a positive impact on any officer's perspective. And that impact will, in turn, impact the competence of the officer and his or her ability to do the job effectively. This then has its effect upon the lives of citizens on the street in the form of engendering a feeling for justice and the rule of law that is not compartmentalized into any one school of thought about what the good in life is.

14-2 Muir and Causing Professionalism

Aside from "being educated" in this general sense, Muir had some important thoughts about police professionalism. He studied a group of young police officers and reflected on how it was possible to engender or to create professionalism in the young officer in particular. As adults we are already formed in some sense and already possess, when we enter the police service, our own individual sets of values, expectations of life, understandings of right and wrong, and personality structures. In other words, we have our character in place. Yet change is possible. Muir talked about how conscious work toward expanding one's practical knowledge and intellectual horizons can enhance one's ability to deal with the moral dilemmas of police work.

Muir talked about three ways in which professionalism could be nurtured. He wrote about language, learning, and leadership. (See box 14-3.)

Box 14-3

Muir's Methods for "Causing Professionalism"

Three factors were emphasized by Muir, not because they are the only ways in which professionalism develops, but because they are clearly factors the police themselves can control. Thus, on the job—after being hired and completing initial academy training—individual officers and police supervisors can work together to engender professionalism by focusing on them:

- Language—Professional police work requires gregariousness, eloquence, and in general the enjoyment of talk.

- Learning—Encouraged by the professional sergeant, police officers need to consistently focus on learning. On-the-job and in the classroom, they must expand their understanding of human nature, the law, and alternative methods of dealing with the problems of their communities and of individual people.

- Leadership—Encouraged by the professional chief and/or upper-level managers, police officers can work in an environment that is safe from outside political influence and is permeated by the understanding that being a competent professional will bring great rewards. On the other hand, incompetence in its many forms will not be tolerated.

When discussing language, Muir focused on the need for police officers to be gregarious or talkative. He suggested that enjoying "chewing the fat" is integral to the job of relating to people and to both understanding and motivating them. Talking and listening to people are a part of the give-and-take of communicating via language. Such communication teaches the intelligent police officer about specific people, about groups of people, about the social atmosphere on a given beat, about people's expectations of the police, and about people's understanding of the good in life.

Experiencing this sort of interaction on a regular basis engenders professionalism by keeping the police in touch with the citizens they serve. But there is more to what Muir is saying. Muir suggests that talking to people involves teaching and persuading them about how to live a good life. Young people in particular are prone to respond, Muir suggests, to intelligent, caring, honest police officers who teach them there is a great deal to be gained by playing by the rules in life. As teachers in a curbside classroom, professional police officers could do more to generate peace and respect for the law and to change the lives of individuals under certain circumstances than could all the rest of society's institutions combined.

Thus, understanding language and using it for good purposes is one way for the professional to get the job done on the street. Of Muir's three points, this is the most critical for our discussion because it is most directly in the hands of each individual police officer.

Muir's other two points deal with a type of learning about competence on the job that is related to the teaching of cops by their sergeants and the leadership of the chief. The learning that stems from the sergeant and the leadership that comes from the chief are important later in the careers of young officers, when they themselves become sergeants and chiefs and their own abilities to engender professionalism, as Muir suggests, are directly related to their abilities as police leaders.

Summary

Final Message   In chapter 14, we have discussed several sets of ideas about how intelligent, professional officers can and must work at continually reinventing themselves. We are back to chapter 7's ideas about working on character. Questioning, adapting, re-evaluating, and learning are at the heart of this effort. To be stagnant, to think that "I have it figured out," is to make a fatal error. No police officer has all the answers and knows exactly how to do it all. No police officer is so intelligent and so experienced that professional growth can cease. This reality defines both the best and the worst dynamics of police work.

One can never stop working on his or her professional body of knowledge and upon his or her craftsmanship. No one is ever "done" with inventing himself or herself as a police officer. This can appear to be a stressful reality because it means there is no slacking off, no time to waste on self-congratulation, no vacations from doing the hard work of self-improvement. But, on the positive side, it makes police work exciting and dynamic. If you are never done learning and reinventing yourself, then you are involved in a job that is never quite the same from day to day.

So here, at the end of our book, one message for readers to take with them is this: Police work is a challenging profession that provides a never-ending sequence of stimulating experiences. Officers who seek to be the best they can be must continuously strive to challenge themselves. No

Box 14-4

Review—Our Ethic to Live By

- Beneficence: The *prima facie* obligation to "do good"
  - Always do good/never do harm
  - Prevent harm/remove harm
- Justice: The obligation to make "equal distribution"
  - Equality of substantive treatment
  - Equality before the law (equality of opportunity)

amount of external motivation will substitute for the personal commitment to grow and to enhance knowledge, skills, and character.

A second message woven throughout the book is that the most appropriate focal point for this growth is our ethic to live by (see box 14-4). In embracing a consistent, relentless awareness of the requirements of the principles of beneficence and distributive justice, police officers not only do good for their communities but also participate in creating dynamic lives for themselves. Cutting through all of the multiple, conflicting, and vague roles required of police officers, these principles provide a beacon toward which police officers can aim all of their efforts and from which they will, in turn, receive direction and sustenance.

This book includes no effort to create lists of do's and don'ts. Police officers do that for themselves. They always have. No matter what amount of academic training or level of experience they may possess, police officers have always made up their own sets of guidelines and practical rules of thumb for handling different types of details. This is perfectly appropriate as long as such self-generated guidelines are never considered to be "finished" and as long as the police officers attempt to focus their ever-changing sets of practical rules on our two over riding principles.

Being a Good Person We have come full circle in this book, back to the idea we suggested in its first pages: To be a competent, professional police officer is to cultivate the moral habits that are necessary to be a good person. There is no divorcing the police role from the individual's role as a person. There is no dividing line that separates the private life from the professional one. A person is not one human being at home and another on the job. He or she is integrated into a whole that the thoughtful, competent professional consciously cultivates.

In seeking to put together the competence necessary to be an effective street cop, the individual officer must possess a large amount of procedural expertise about how to be a cop in the practical sense. Then, too, substantive knowledge about the law, crime causation, and the criminal justice system's process is indispensable. Finally, a practical, working understanding of how a given police department works and of the expectations of a given community and its neighborhoods must round out the tremendous volume of information and skills possessed by the competent officer.

The glue that holds all of this together is the police officer's personal ethical perspective. Police work is all about character. Without an understanding of the ethical implications of the job, and without possessing the ability to solve ethical dilemmas for others, the police officer is lost in a sea of bits and pieces of knowledge that lack integration. To put it all together and become today's competent, professional officer is to possess this body of knowledge and to integrate it with an understanding of what it means to be a good person, to live a good life, and to be an ethical officer. These two entities—the body of knowledge and the ethical perspective—are worthless without each other.

Topics for Discussion

1. Consider the authors' argument that at least some college education is important for all police officers. Discuss how the theory of the classroom can be applied to the practical realities of life on the street. What do you think of the axiom that a college education is not necessary because "you can't learn police work from a book"?

2. Refer to box 14-3 and Muir's reflections on what makes a competent, professional officer. When discussing "language," he wrote that teaching and persuading people is a big part of the job. Discuss how being the "strong, silent type" of police officer is a mistake as it alienates the officer from people and from life on the beat.

3. Other than taking some college classes, what types of non-police-related experiences, hobbies, and avocations might help to make a police officer develop, grow, and become more competent? Discuss why it is so important to stay in touch with "other-than-police-subcultural" ways of thinking and to cultivate civilians as friends.

Bibliographical Essay

This essay is presented for the reader interested in following up on the various topics in our text. It briefly outlines some important books written in the fields through which we have traveled. We divide this piece into three areas of interest. First, we will talk about books written by sociologists and political scientists about the police in general. Second, we will list introductory texts that might be used to pursue an interest in the philosophers to which we have referred. Finally, the field of criminal justice ethics and police ethics in particular will be discussed.

I. Police Work Generally

A good reference book about the police, one which has been updated several times since its original publication in 1967, is Jerome Skolnick's *Justice Without Trial, 3rd Ed.* (New York, 1994). This work will give the reader a feel for how earlier sociologists viewed the study of the police. A good textbook on the police and police systems, one of the most widely used in America, is Samuel Walker's *The Police in America, 3rd Ed.* (New York, 1999). Both of these classic works will ground the reader in an understanding of how the police are viewed and analyzed by academics.

In this text, we have often referred to William K. Muir Jr.'s work, *Police: Streetcorner Politicians* (Chicago, 1977). The reader may very well want to go to the original source to experience Muir's ideas directly. This book, one of the most insightful works ever done on the police, in our opinion, explains Muir's ideas about coercive power, professionalism, and developing character.

Carl Klockars, again someone whom we have cited several times in this work, wrote The *Idea of Police* (Newbury Park, Calif., 1985) in an effort to produce a short work for students in the field. This piece discusses the role and functions of the police.

For an analysis of the police subculture, a central topic for those interested in this field, see John Crank's *Understanding Police Culture* (Cincinnati, 1998). It is not only an important work in itself, but it exposes the reader to the entire field of study today—citing many authors, theories, and pieces of research.

A good collection of essays on various topics relating to police work—including James W. Wilson and George Kelling's now-famous "Broken Windows," one of the works that spawned the community-based policing movement—is Steven Brandl and David Barlow's *Classics in Policing* (Cincinnati, 1996). The reader interested in the roots of community-based policing (CBP) should also read Herman Goldstein's *Problem-Oriented Policing* (New York, 1990), a book that is largely given credit for the ideas and ideals behind CBP.

II. Philosophy

A good introductory text in the field of ethics in general is S. Hampshire's *Freedom of the Individual* (New York, 1959). For an historical treatment of the development of moral philosophy—from Aristotle through Kant and Mill to the present day—read Alisdair MacIntyre's *A Short History of Ethics* (New York, 1966). This is an important work by one of today's most influential philosophers.

To investigate Aristotle and the principles of virtue-based ethics (and character) read Marjorie Grene's *A Portrait of Aristotle* (London, 1963). Or for a shorter, clear, highly readable approach to Aristotle, read W.D. Ross's *Aristotle* (Oxford, 1930), considered by many to be the best treatment of the great man ever written.

The best introductory explanation of the philosophy of Kant, written in a very short and readable way, is Stephen Korner's *Kant* (New York, 1955). For exploring Mill (and Bentham) and the utilitarian field, read B. William's and J.J.C. Smart's *Utilitarianism: For and Against* (Cambridge, 1973). Each of these works provides a more readily understandable and useful view of these ideas than most readers would develop if they read the philosophers' original works.

III. Police Ethics

Joycelyn Pollock wrote *Ethics in Crime and Justice* (Belmont, Calif., 1998), to which we have made reference in several places. This work discusses in greater detail the philosophical perspectives to which we have referred. It also includes numerous other schools of thought, such as those of natural law, religion, and the ethics of care in a way our short work has not. Pollock sets up her philosophical perspectives and then applies them in a step-by-step manner to all areas of the criminal justice field, not just to the police.

Victor Kappelar, Richard Sluder, and Geoffrey Alpert wrote *Forces of Deviance* (Prospect Heights, Ill., 1998), which discusses police deviance in depth. This book includes within its arguments a discussion of the work of Gary Sykes and David Matza on deviance in general, something that we alluded to in chapter 10. John Crank and Michael Caldero's work, *Police Ethics: The Corruption of Noble Cause* (Cincinnati, 2000), is an important, in-depth treatment of one type of police misconduct. Finally, the debate about which method of police review is best, internal affairs or civilian review, is treated in Douglas Perez's *Common Sense About Police Review* (Philadelphia, 1994).

Index